4B OG

Also from EATMS Productions

Books on power, survival, women's autonomy, and the systems shaping modern America.

Nonfiction

Billionaires, Capitalism, and Power

Evil and the Mountain Ungreed
Self Help for American Billionaires
Selfish Steve and the Ivory Tower
Tariffs, Taxes, & Face-Eating Leopards
Ban Billionaires: Fascism Fix

Fascism, Religion, and Cultural Control

Self Help for the Manosphere
Fascism 2025
Fascism & the Perverts & the Greed Virus
Christian Fascism Marriage Book
Tyranny, Table Manners, & Tiramisu

Guides for Women's Autonomy and Protection

How to Survive in Post-America as a Woman
Project 2025 American Drag
4B – Burn, Ban, Boycott, Build
4B OG – So No Go GYN
I'm Glad He's Dead

Analysis of Authoritarian Project 2025

Project 2025: The Blueprint
Project 2025: The List
Project 2025, Christian Dumb Dumbs, & The Republican Agenda
Fascism, Project 2025, & The Pinkprint

Modern Rewrites for Women

Stoic Principles Reimagined
Siddhartha Reimagined
The Prince Reimagined for Women
The Art of War Reimagined for Women
The Jungle Reimagined
The Constitution Reimagined for Women

Machine Learning Series

AI, Bitcoin, Nostr for Women
AI, Safety, & Security for Women
AI, Anxiety, & Health for Women
AI, Kids, & Family Safety for Women
AI, Creativity, & Personal Expression for Women
AI, Independent Work, & Parallel Power for Women

Social Systems Series

Emotional Labor for Women
Household Power for Women
Workplace Power for Women
Medical Bias for Women
Aging Systems for Women
Recovery Systems for Women

Fiction

Dystopian Stories of Resistance and Collapse

Propaganda Paige & the Missing Prosperity
Propaganda Paige & the TIDE Manifesto
Propaganda Paige & the Shadow Cartographers
Propaganda Paige & the Prosperity Alliance
Propaganda Paige & the Shattered Truth
Propaganda Paige & the Rising TIDE
Propaganda Paige & the Last Bastion
Propaganda Paige & the Dawn of Prosperity
Project 2025: Dorian — The Last Men
Project 2025: Boy — A Last Men Novel

4B OG
SO NO GO GYN

Inspired by the South Koren Movement 4B

by
Esme Mees
& Petra Nein

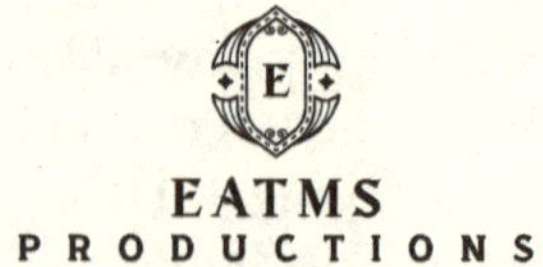

This title is part of an ongoing body of work. All EATMS Productions titles, across all series, authors, and formats, are components of a single connected project.

This book is a work of opinion and creative interpretation. While some names and events may be referenced or alluded to, any claims made are based on publicly available information and are intended as satire, parody, or commentary on societal and political issues. The content should not be interpreted as factual assertions about any individual or entity. The author does not intend to defraud, defame, or mislead, and encourages readers to form their own conclusions. Any resemblance to real persons, living or dead, is purely coincidental unless explicitly noted otherwise.

ISBN 978-1-966014-11-9

Cover, interior design, interior prints by: Esme Mees

eatms@pm.me
www.eatms.me

Check out EATMS Underground:
https://tinyurl.com/eatmsNOSTR

Printed in the United States of America.

Search www.reprodcutiverights.gov

Yep, it's gone. Fools are systematically dismantling the government, and they'll get to you and me very soon.

Now, delete your period-tracking apps, stop sharing **any** private information online, and seriously consider unplugging from all anti-privacy, anti-freedom "socials."

— Common Sense

Table of Contents

Acknowledgment

The Women Who Showed Us the Way

Before we begin, we give thanks to the women of South Korea, the originators of the 4B movement, no dating, no sex, no marriage, no childbirth, who saw the writing on the wall long before many of us did. These women did not wait for permission to say no. They did not waste time begging men to be better. They withdrew their labor, their bodies, their energy, because they knew the truth: men will not change unless they are forced to.

Korea's 4B movement was born out of necessity, in a society where women were expected to sacrifice everything while men refused to change. It was a radical act of survival, not just protest. It was a declaration that women do not exist for men's benefit, and that women's autonomy is non-negotiable.

Now, it's America's turn.

Because our men are no better, in fact, they may be worse. They are rapists, pedophiles, wife-beaters, abusers, incels, porn addicts, and power-hungry tyrants who openly legislate their control over our bodies. They tell us to shut up and take it while elevating the worst among them to rule over us. Enough.

The women of Korea led the way. Now, we join them. Or rather, we opt out.

Introduction

Welcome to the New Gilead. It Happened While You Were Looking

They wouldn't really do that. Yes, they would, and they did. They told us we were hysterical, overreacting, making things up. They called us alarmists when we warned that they wouldn't stop at Roe v. Wade, that birth control would be next, that they'd criminalize pregnancy, jail doctors, hunt down women crossing state lines, revive centuries-old laws to ban abortion pills, and even prosecute miscarriages. And then, they did exactly that. There was no negotiation, no pause for reflection, no shame, just a relentless, calculated stripping away of rights. The ruling class, led by rapists, pedophiles, and Christofascist authoritarians, made their intentions clear: they don't care if we die. The cruelty is the point. Women in 2025 have fewer rights than their mothers and grandmothers, and if we don't stop them, our daughters will have none at all.

The slow creep of fascism didn't come with jackboots and torchlight parades. It came through state legislatures, through Supreme Court rulings, through men in suits quoting the Bible as they passed laws that erased women from the legal category of personhood. It came in whispers at first, a decision here, a policy there, a handful of judges appointed by a serial rapist who lost the popular vote. It came as bills restricting abortion to six weeks, then total bans, then bounty hunting laws deputizing citizens to snitch on desperate women trying to escape red-state borders. It came with the criminalization of healthcare, with hospital administrators forcing doctors to let women rot with sepsis rather than intervene before the fetal heartbeat stopped. It came in states where even life-threatening pregnancies became death sentences, where lawmakers debated whether a woman actively dying in a hospital bed should be given care if it meant terminating a nonviable pregnancy. And it came in the silence that followed, when those who once said "they would never go that far" refused to acknowledge what was happening in front of them.

Roe was never the finish line for them. It was the beginning. The minute the ink dried on that Supreme Court ruling, they dusted off the Comstock Act of 1873, a Victorian-era law banning the mailing of "obscene" materials, including information about contraception and abortion. A law that had been considered a relic of the past, unenforceable in a modern democracy, was suddenly back in play. They started banning abortion pills, restricting telemedicine, forcing pharmacies to refuse life-saving medication under threat of prosecution. Women in blue states told themselves they were safe, that it couldn't happen there, as judges installed by fascists began floating national abortion bans, interstate extraditions, and the criminalization of anyone aiding a woman in obtaining medical care. Government websites that once provided reproductive health information were scrubbed overnight, helplines for abortion access shut down, resources erased as if they had never existed. It wasn't enough to take away the right to choose; they had to erase the knowledge that choice ever existed at all.

The playbook is not new. It is the same one used by every theocratic state in history, force women into submission through legal, economic, and social means until they are too broken to fight back. First, they come for reproductive rights, then for contraception, then for divorce laws, then for women's ability to leave the home without permission. The war against women is not a series of isolated incidents but a coordinated effort, a deliberate strategy to roll back the clock to a time when women were property, when we had no say over our bodies, our futures, or our lives. The rise of Christian nationalism is not a coincidence. It is the foundation of their movement, the ideological justification for every attack on women's rights. Obey. Submit. Die. That is the message, whether spoken aloud or embedded in every law they pass.

And yet, they still expect us not to notice. They mock us, gaslight us, tell us we are imagining things. They elevate rapists to the highest courts in the land, protect pedophiles in their ranks, praise domestic abusers and turn them into governors, senators, and presidents. They smirk as they strip away our rights, laughing as we are told to "just move to another state" as if state borders will hold when federal bans come down. They tell us to be grateful that we are not living in the Middle East, even as they implement policies that mirror the worst authoritarian regimes. They dare us to resist, knowing full well that peaceful protest means nothing to a system that no longer even pretends to value democracy. They have the courts, the cops, the corporations, the churches, and they are coming for everything.

This is not politics. This is survival. This is not about policy debates or compromise or finding common ground with those who see us as breeding stock. This is war. And the only option left is to refuse. To cut them off from every avenue of power, to starve them of what they believe they are entitled to, to make their lives as empty and miserable as they have tried to make ours. The 4B movement is not a protest. It is the last defense. No more dating, no more sex, no more marriage, no more babies. If they want to rule over us, let them do it without the benefit of our bodies, our labor, our care. Let them wither under the weight of their own misogyny, isolated and alone, while we build a world without them. Because the truth is, we don't need them. They need us. And it's time they learned what that really means.

Rapists, Pedophiles, and Abusers – The Men They Choose to Rule Us

Why is every powerful man an open predator? Why does every headline about another politician, another judge, another CEO, another billionaire seem to reveal the same grotesque reality, that the people in power are not just complicit in male violence, but the perpetrators of it? This is not coincidence.

This is not a series of unfortunate bad apples. This is a system functioning exactly as designed, a world built to reward and elevate the worst men while grinding everyone else underfoot. Abusers don't just exist in power. They are placed there on purpose.

From the White House to the Supreme Court, from Congress to the governor's mansion, the men making the laws that govern our bodies, our rights, and our lives all share a common trait: they view women as objects, not people. They are not just anti-woman ideologues; they are men with long histories of violence against women, men with credible rape accusations, men who have been caught on tape bragging about sexual assault, men who have been credibly accused of molesting children, beating their wives, coercing mistresses into abortions, and getting away with it because the entire system exists to protect them. They are not anomalies. They are the rule.

Look at the lineup. Donald Trump, who openly bragged about grabbing women by the pussy, has been accused of sexual misconduct by more than twenty women, including a rape conviction in civil court. Brett Kavanaugh, who cried and screamed his way onto the Supreme Court after multiple women accused him of sexual assault, now sits in a lifetime position deciding the fate of those very same women. Roy Moore, a man banned from his local mall for preying on teenage girls, was nearly elected to the Senate in Alabama because for many voters, his predation was a feature, not a bug. Clarence Thomas, who harassed Anita Hill with grotesque sexual comments in the workplace, now sits on the highest court in the land, helping to strip women of their rights decades later. These men are not outliers. They are the blueprint.

They didn't even try to hide it. They didn't have to. Every time another predator was exposed, the response was not shame or accountability, but defiance. These men were protected, defended, even celebrated. Their supporters laughed in our faces, mocked the survivors, declared their rapists to be good men under attack by the evil forces of feminism. The louder women screamed, the harder they pushed these men to the top, ensuring that the institutions governing us would be permanently tainted by the worst of them. And for what? Why would they rally around the most vile men among them? Because they know that a man who has been credibly accused of rape, sexual harassment, or domestic violence will never stand up for women. A man with blood on his hands will always vote against the rights of women because his own survival depends on keeping us powerless.

This is the protection racket of male violence. Every man in power who has raped, assaulted, or beaten a woman knows that the system is on his side because it was built by men exactly like him. Rapists cover for rapists. Abusers shield abusers. The network of male power is designed not only to keep them safe, but to ensure that they are the ones writing the laws, handing down the rulings, and deciding who gets justice and who is silenced. It is no accident that women are forced to give birth in states run by men who have mistreated women their entire lives. It is no coincidence that domestic abusers are more likely to get custody of their children in family court. It is no surprise that a Supreme Court packed with accused sexual predators voted to revoke women's rights. This is not an unfortunate side effect. It is the entire point.

And still, they have the audacity to tell us to calm down. To be reasonable. To trust the process. As if the process wasn't built to protect the monsters who see us as disposable. As if the deck wasn't stacked against us from the start. As if we are too stupid to see exactly what is happening right in front of us. They elevate the worst of men because the worst of men will always do their bidding. They put rapists on the highest court in the land because rapists will always vote against women's autonomy. They let predators run for office because predators will always ensure that women remain trapped, silenced, and unable to fight back.

The message is clear. They are telling us, in every way possible, that we do not matter. That our lives, our voices, our safety, our autonomy are all secondary to protecting their own. That they will continue elevating rapists and abusers to the highest levels of power, and there is nothing we can do about it.

They think we will accept this. They think we will be afraid, exhausted, beaten down into submission. They think we will keep playing by their rules, that we will beg and plead for mercy while they laugh in our faces. But they are wrong. We see them. We see what they are doing. We see the system they have built, the laws they have twisted, the game they have rigged. And we are done playing.

They Think We're Too Dumb to Notice – The Ultimate Gaslight

They think we'll keep falling for it, that we'll keep playing along, that we'll keep believing this is all some kind of misunderstanding, a policy debate, an unfortunate side effect of democracy in action. They think they can keep moving the goalposts, keep lying to our faces, keep gaslighting us into submission while they strip away our rights, one by one, until there is nothing left. They think we won't fight back because they have spent generations convincing us that we are powerless. They think we are too exhausted, too afraid, too distracted to recognize what they are doing in real time. But we see them. And we are done.

They're coming for birth control next. How many times did we say it? How many times did we warn them? We were called hysterical, alarmist, irrational, accused of overreacting, of making a big deal out of nothing. "No one is banning contraception," they scoffed, as they laid the groundwork to do exactly that. We watched as they stripped abortion rights state by state, and when we pointed out that the very same people attacking abortion access had also spent years trying to block birth control, they told us we were crazy. And yet, here we are.

Supreme Court justices openly questioning whether Griswold v. Connecticut, the ruling that gave women the right to birth control in the first place, should be overturned. Republican legislators drafting bills to make IUDs and Plan B illegal. Pharmacists refusing to fill prescriptions for contraception under the guise of "religious freedom." Insurance companies rolling back coverage for reproductive healthcare while anti-choice groups push for bans on everything from emergency contraception to in-vitro fertilization. They told us they only wanted to ban abortion, but it was never just about abortion. It was always about control.

And it doesn't stop at contraception. The attack on women's autonomy is expanding with terrifying speed, targeting not just reproductive rights but every avenue of independence women have fought for. Divorce laws are under attack in red states, with lawmakers openly musing about banning no-fault divorce, making it harder for women to escape abusive marriages. Conservative judges are reviving archaic interpretations of "head of household" laws, suggesting that a husband's permission should be required for a wife's financial decisions. And then there's the looming crackdown on women's movement itself, state legislators proposing travel bans for pregnant women, laws requiring women to prove they aren't seeking an abortion before they are allowed to leave their home state. The blueprint is clear. First, they strip away our right to medical care, then our right to financial independence, then our right to leave at all. They are building the legal framework for a new kind of captivity, brick by brick, case by case, ruling by ruling, and they are betting that we are too distracted to stop them before it is too late.

The demand for women's silence has always been part of the plan. Every woman who has ever spoken up, who has ever named her abuser, who has ever dared to demand justice has been met with the same response: shut up. Be quiet. Stop complaining. Move on. We watched as the #MeToo movement was dismissed as a "witch hunt," as powerful men were momentarily inconvenienced and then rewarded with book deals, comeback tours, and new jobs in the same industries that supposedly blacklisted them. We were told that cancel culture had gone too far, that we needed to be fair to men whose lives were being "ruined" by accusations, while the actual survivors were pushed out of their jobs, their careers derailed, their safety threatened. The backlash was swift and brutal, a deliberate campaign to reassert male dominance, to make it clear that there would be consequences for any woman who dared to hold men accountable. And now we are right back where we started, with the powerful more untouchable than ever, with rapists in the highest offices, with domestic abusers writing our laws, with misogynists making policy decisions about our bodies while we are told to smile and be grateful that we still have the right to complain at all.

Meanwhile, in Texas, they have gone one step further. They have turned their citizens into bounty hunters, deputizing them to track down and punish women who seek medical care. They have passed laws that allow private individuals to sue anyone who "aids and abets" an abortion, doctors, nurses, clinic staff, even an Uber driver who takes a woman to an appointment. They have created a system where neighbors are encouraged to turn on each other, where people can profit off the suffering of women, where abortion bans are enforced not by the state, but by a network of informants eager to cash in on a $10,000 payout. They call this "pro-life." It is nothing but state-sanctioned terror.

They think we don't see what they are doing. They think they can keep tightening the noose, little by little, hoping we won't notice until it is too late. They think they can ban abortion, then birth control, then divorce, then travel, then financial independence, then speech itself, and that we will simply accept it. They think we are stupid, complacent, too caught up in the day-to-day struggle of survival to recognize the full scale of the war being waged against us. But we see them. We see exactly what they are doing. And we will not be silent.

The abortion witch hunts have begun, and they are not stopping until every pregnant person is under their control. This is not about life. This is not about babies. This is about power, about punishment, about making sure that women know there is no escape. They have turned pregnancy into a life sentence, a means of control so absolute that even rape, even incest, even life-threatening medical emergencies are no longer considered justifications for intervention. They want women to suffer, to be trapped, to die if necessary, because their goal was never to protect life, it was to enforce submission.

Rape, incest, forced birth, this is the nightmare of pregnancy under their rule. A 10-year-old girl raped by a family member is now expected to carry a pregnancy to term. A teenager assaulted by her stepfather is told that the child inside her matters more than she does. A woman attacked by a stranger is forced to bear her rapist's offspring because the men in power have decided that her trauma is irrelevant, that her suffering is a price they are willing to pay for their theocratic vision. It is not just happening in one state, or under one law, or because of one ruling. This is the logical endpoint of the entire anti-abortion movement. They have created a system where the rapist has more rights than his victim, where the state protects the predator over the survivor, where a fetus is granted legal status while the woman carrying it is stripped of her humanity. And they do not care.

In hospitals across the country, women are bleeding out while doctors refuse to treat them out of fear. Pregnant people in medical crisis are being told to wait in parking lots until their condition worsens enough that doctors can legally intervene. Women with nonviable pregnancies are forced to carry dead fetuses inside them for weeks, risking sepsis, hemorrhage, and death because medical professionals are too terrified of prosecution to act. In Texas, in Florida, in Missouri, in every red state that has criminalized abortion, physicians are being forced to choose between their oath to save lives and their fear of being sued, arrested, or losing their license. And so, women die. This is not accidental. This is policy. When they passed these laws, they knew exactly what would happen. They knew that banning abortion without exceptions meant that pregnant people would suffer and die. And they did it anyway.

The Death of Feminism or the Birth of Something Stronger?

For decades, women were told that the fight was over. That we had won. That feminism had achieved its goals and anything beyond that was just whining, unnecessary, outdated. The Equal Pay Act, Title IX, Roe v. Wade, women in the workplace, women in Congress, women CEOs, what else could we possibly want? We were mocked for continuing to push, told we were tilting at windmills, called man-haters, radicals, shrill, bitter. The message was clear: shut up and be grateful. Stop talking about sexism. Stop talking about violence. Stop talking about power.

And for a time, it almost worked. Women, lulled into a false sense of progress, began to believe that things were moving forward. That the clock would never roll backward, that legal rights were permanent, that no one would dare undo decades of hard-won gains. We believed the lie because we wanted to believe it. Because the alternative, that the fight was far from over, was too exhausting, too terrifying, too demoralizing to accept. But they never stopped fighting against us. They were never content to let us have our sliver of autonomy, our fragile, conditional place in the world. They were patient. They waited. They let us get comfortable. And then, when they had enough power, when the courts were stacked, when the legislatures were red, when the voters were complacent, they struck.

One by one, they unraveled every supposed guarantee. The right to abortion? Gone. Birth control? Next on the chopping block. Domestic violence protections? Weakening by the day. Pay equity? Still a joke. Maternal health? Worse than ever. In the span of a few years, they erased decades of so-called progress, proving that nothing was ever secure, that every gain was conditional, that without constant vigilance, without relentless opposition, they would take everything back. And now, we are living in the aftermath, in the ruins of the illusion that we had won.

For young women, this is their awakening. They have been forced into a new, dystopian reality before they even had the chance to believe in something better. They are growing up in a world where their rights are fewer than their mothers' and grandmothers', where they can be denied birth control, denied medical care, forced into pregnancies they didn't choose, where they are watching rapists and abusers dictate the laws that govern their bodies. They are not naive. They are not optimistic. They are angry. And they are beginning to understand what women before them tried to warn: there is no such thing as equality when the other side refuses to play fair. They never wanted equality. They never even considered it. They wanted control, and now they have it.

So what now? Do we mourn the death of feminism, or do we create something stronger? Something more radical, more unrelenting, more unwilling to compromise? Because compromise got us here. Good faith got us here. The idea that we could appeal to reason, that we could change their minds, that we could "convince" men to see us as equals, that delusion cost us everything. The 4B doctrine is no longer an idea, no longer a strategy, no longer a theory. It is survival. If we want our power back, we must cut them off from everything. No more sex. No more dating. No more marriage. No more babies. No more emotional labor, no more unpaid work, no more begging for a seat at a table they built to exclude us.

There is nothing left to negotiate. They have shown us, in every way possible, that they will not stop. That they will take and take until we have nothing left, until we are legally, economically, and biologically trapped. We have one option. One response. One weapon they cannot steal, cannot legislate away, cannot criminalize. Us. Our refusal. Our absence. Let them rule over themselves. Let them wither without us. Let them learn what a world without women truly looks like. They need us. We do not need them. And it's time they learned the difference.

The Last Warning – We Are Done Asking

Women have tried everything else. We organized. We protested. We voted. We marched. We wrote letters. We lobbied. We sat through debates, town halls, panel discussions, all while men smirked at us, talked over us, ignored us. We made logical arguments, we provided facts, we exposed injustice, we worked within the system, believing that if we just played by the rules, if we just presented our case reasonably enough, we would be heard. And what did they do? They laughed. They stripped our rights anyway.

They never had any intention of listening. They never saw us as equals. They let us believe we had won something just long enough to make it hurt when they took it all away. They let us believe we had power while they spent decades making sure they could take it back the second they had the chance. And now, they are daring us to fight back. They think we won't. They think we will keep pleading, keep explaining, keep trying to convince them that we deserve basic human rights. But we are done with all of it.

Men will either learn, or they will be left behind. No more pleading. No more explaining. No more convincing. No more waiting for them to evolve, no more hand-holding, no more patience. We do not need to prove anything to them. We do not need their approval to take back what is ours. They are on notice. No more dates. No more sex. No more marriage. No more babies. They will not get access to our bodies, our labor, our care, our time, or our futures. The world they are building is a world without women, and we are going to let them live in it.

Welcome to the 4B strike. We are taking back our power. The era of male entitlement is over. They took everything from us, and now we are taking ourselves away from them. This is not a protest. This is not a request. This is not a warning. This is how we win.

Section 1
Do Not Date Men – Starve the Market

~1
The Cruelty Is the Point
Dating as a Rigged Game

Dating is a rigged game. Women always lose, and men always benefit. They designed it that way. From the moment girls are old enough to understand social roles, they are taught that their value lies in how desirable they are to men. They are groomed to be agreeable, accommodating, forgiving. They are told that their standards are too high, that they need to "give men a chance," that they should smile more, be softer, be more patient. They are gaslit into believing that male entitlement to their time, their energy, and their bodies is just the natural order of things. And so, they enter the dating world already at a disadvantage, trained to tolerate bad behavior, to downplay red flags, to accept the unacceptable.

Men, on the other hand, are conditioned to believe that access to women is their right. That their flaws, their failures, their emotional immaturity will all be fixed by the right woman. That love, sex, and companionship are things they are owed simply for existing. The dating economy has never been about mutual respect or fairness, it is about men taking and women giving. It is about women performing emotional labor while men get to be emotionally stunted. It is about men getting to be selfish, while women are expected to be self-sacrificing. It is about women lowering their standards while men raise their expectations. And when women finally refuse to play along? When they decide they would rather be alone than settle for mediocrity? The backlash is swift and vicious.

Because dating is not just a game, it is an indoctrination system. It normalizes misogyny at every level. It rewards men for being arrogant, unkind, emotionally unavailable, even openly abusive, while punishing women for having boundaries, expectations, or self-respect. Women who reject bad men are called bitter. Women who expect basic human decency are told they are asking for too much. Women who refuse to settle are accused of being delusional, of being past their prime, of dying alone with their cats. But a man can be an unwashed, unemployed, 40-year-old who plays video games in his mother's basement, and he will still feel entitled to a 22-year-old supermodel who will cook, clean, and provide unlimited sex. Women are expected to work for love, to suffer for it, to earn it. Men simply believe they deserve it.

But what happens when we withdraw? What happens when we stop playing along? What happens when women collectively refuse to engage? We have seen glimpses of it already, men whining on podcasts about women not wanting them anymore, men panicking about the rise of "passport bros" because they can no longer find women at home who will tolerate them, men screaming into the void about "feminism ruining relationships" because women now realize they are better off single. The moment women stop giving, men start losing. The moment women say no, men realize how little they actually bring to the table.

And that is why they are panicking. That is why they double down on shaming women, on trying to guilt-trip them back into submission, on making marriage harder to leave, on rolling back reproductive rights, on making sure that women cannot opt out of the system. They know that their entire world relies on women continuing to play along, to settle, to tolerate, to suffer. They know that if women were truly free to choose, most of them would choose to walk away.

So, we walk. We refuse. We step back and let them drown in their own mediocrity. Let them deal with the loneliness they claimed we would suffer. Let them feel the absence of the women they took for granted. Let them realize, too late, that we were the only thing keeping their world running. They thought they could control us, that they could gaslight us into submission, that they could bully us into obedience. They forgot one crucial thing: we don't need them. They need us. And now, we are gone.

How Dating Normalizes Misogyny

How dating normalizes misogyny starts early. Long before a girl ever goes on her first date, she has already been primed for the imbalance. She has already learned that boys pulling her hair and teasing her is "flirting." That her comfort and boundaries come second to their feelings. That saying no too firmly makes her mean, while saying yes to something she doesn't want makes her agreeable, likable, nice. She is told to be accommodating, to be patient, to give second chances. She is taught that boys will be boys, that men need time to mature, that she should lower her standards because expecting too much will only leave her disappointed. From childhood, she is conditioned to prioritize men over herself.

By the time she enters the dating world, the rules are already set. She will be the one planning dates, managing emotions, keeping conversations going. She will be the one navigating men's fragile egos, tiptoeing around their insecurities, avoiding rejection that might turn violent. She will be told she needs to prove herself, to impress him, to show that she is worth his time. He, on the other hand, will simply show up. He will expect to be adored for the bare minimum. He will demand her attention, her affection, her energy, and if she hesitates, he will call her difficult, high-maintenance, ungrateful.

The modern dating world is not just toxic, it is a carefully constructed system designed to keep women in a permanent state of self-doubt and overperformance. It is why dating apps are flooded with men who put zero effort into their profiles but still believe they deserve beautiful, successful, high-achieving women. It is why the most mediocre men believe they are a "catch" while women are told they need to settle before it's too late. It is why when a woman says she is not interested in dating, she is met with anger, confusion, and hostility, because her refusal is not seen as personal preference, but as an attack on the entire male entitlement structure.

This is why every woman has a story about rejecting a man and paying the price for it. The man who insulted her for not giving him her number. The one who followed her home. The one who called her a bitch, a whore, a gold digger. The one who accused her of leading him on for simply existing in his vicinity. The one who snapped, who lashed out, who could not accept that she was not interested. Because the moment a woman asserts her own desires, her own choices, her own autonomy, she disrupts the entire social order that tells men they are owed her time, her body, her compliance. And that is why they fight so hard to maintain the illusion that dating is just a game, a fun and harmless tradition. Because if women start seeing it for what it really is, a system of control, not companionship, they might finally decide to stop playing.

And that is the greatest threat of all. Not feminism, not progress, not even equality. The greatest threat to men who believe they are owed women's attention is the possibility that women might wake up one day and realize they don't need men at all. That they could be free, happy, and successful on their own. That they could reject relationships altogether and live their lives without catering to male expectations. That they could refuse to be someone's girlfriend, someone's wife, someone's backup plan. That they could simply be.

And that is why they are panicking. That is why every dating "expert" warns women not to wait too long, not to be too picky, not to stay single past their "prime." That is why men on social media rage about "modern women," about feminism, about how dating is ruined because women won't just obey anymore. They don't actually want love. They don't want connection. They want compliance. And when they realize they aren't getting it, they don't reflect, they don't change, they don't improve. They double down. They punish. They lash out.

Because if women stop playing the game, the entire system collapses. And that terrifies them.

What Happens When We Withdraw?

The withdrawal of women from a system that has never served them is not just an act of defiance; it is an act of survival. It is the inevitable response to a world that has demanded everything from women while offering nothing in return. For centuries, men built a social order in which they assumed perpetual access to women, our labor, our time, our bodies, our devotion. They assumed that no matter how little they gave, no matter how poorly they behaved, no matter how deeply they failed, there would always be a woman willing to endure, to make excuses, to carry the burden of love on her shoulders. That world no longer exists.

Women are not waiting anymore. They are not pleading, not compromising, not bending themselves to fit into a mold that was never designed for them. They are not playing a game that was always rigged against them, a game where they were told to be less, to expect less, to settle for whatever scraps of affection, attention, and commitment a man was willing to toss their way. And this refusal, this exodus, has sent men into a spiral. The moment women stop giving, the entire structure of male entitlement collapses. And so, men rage. They rage at the women who walk away. They rage at the women who raise their standards. They rage at the women who choose their own lives over the thankless work of maintaining a relationship with a man who refuses to meet them halfway. They rage, not because they care, not because they love, but because they were never taught to exist without women doing the emotional labor of their lives.

This is why their responses are so predictable, so repetitive, so unoriginal. They mock women for being alone while simultaneously lamenting their own loneliness. They complain that women are too independent, too educated, too unwilling to settle while simultaneously whining that they cannot find anyone to date. They flee to other countries, looking for women who have fewer options, who have been economically and socially trapped into the same compliance that women in the West have abandoned. They speak of a crisis, of population collapse, of the "end of civilization" as if civilization itself was ever dependent on men keeping women trapped. They create laws to try to force women back into submission, restricting reproductive rights, penalizing single mothers, making divorce harder, all in an attempt to undo the shift that has already begun. But they cannot stop it.

Because this is not about individual men failing to find love, it is about an entire gender realizing that they were never meant to be the default. That their presence in women's lives was never a necessity, but an expectation enforced through economic dependence, religious doctrine, and social stigma. Now that those levers of control are failing, men have nothing left but anger. And that anger is misplaced. They should not be angry at the women who left. They should be angry at the system that raised them to believe they never had to try, that they never had to be more than the bare minimum, that women would always be waiting for them, no matter how deeply they failed to evolve.

So now, they can sit in the world they built, a world where they were always at the center, where they were told from birth that women would orbit around them, that no matter how little they contributed, they would always be desired, always be chosen, always be accommodated. They can feel the emptiness of their own choices, the hollowness of their own existence, now that the women they took for granted have removed themselves from the equation. They can wrestle with the weight of their own entitlement, realizing too late that the system they upheld was not built to sustain them, that it only functioned because women were there, carrying the invisible labor, shouldering the responsibility, bending themselves to make it all work. Now, left to their own devices, they see how little they have to offer, how unprepared they are to live without women's constant emotional, domestic, and social labor smoothing out the rough edges of their lives. They can rage into the void about how unfair it all is, about how women have become too selfish, too independent, too unwilling to settle. They can cry about loneliness, about declining marriage rates, about the fact that fewer and fewer women are willing to sacrifice their autonomy for a relationship that only benefits one side. But it will change nothing.

The moment of reckoning has already passed. Women are not listening anymore. Women are not interested in their complaints, their frustrations, their desperate attempts to claw back relevance in a world that no longer caters to them. Women are not coming back. And this, more than anything, is what terrifies them. They thought we would always be there. They thought that no matter how badly they behaved, how little they grew, how much they took without giving, women would remain. They assumed that we had no other choice, that we would continue to accept the bare minimum, that we would continue to shrink ourselves, to silence ourselves, to prioritize them above all else. But now, they know the truth. We don't need them. They need us. And now, we are gone.

~2

The Industry of Male Entitlement

From Dating Apps to Arranged Marriages – How Society Traps Women

The industry of male entitlement does not merely exist, it permeates every layer of society, shaping expectations, laws, and entire economies to ensure that men never have to confront their own irrelevance. It is not enough that men desire access to women; they have ensured that this access is embedded into the very structure of culture itself, making it nearly impossible for women to escape without consequence. From the earliest moments of childhood, girls are indoctrinated into the belief that their worth is contingent on being chosen, that their success is measured in how well they fulfill men's expectations. Boys, in contrast, are raised with the assurance that women will always be available to them, that companionship, sex, and emotional labor are not privileges to be earned but entitlements that society has guaranteed them. This is why, when faced with rejection, true, collective rejection, men react not with self-reflection but with rage, confusion, and demands for systemic intervention to force women back into compliance.

This industry of entitlement stretches far beyond the realm of personal relationships. It is not simply about dating or marriage, it is about the way the entire infrastructure of society has been built to accommodate men's desires while ensuring women's dependency. The economy thrives on women's unpaid labor, on their willingness to take on the lowest-paid, most precarious jobs while still shouldering the burden of childcare, elder care, and domestic work. The political system is designed to keep women occupied with personal survival, fighting for reproductive rights, for fair wages, for legal protections, so that they do not have the time or power to fundamentally challenge the structure itself. Religious and cultural institutions reinforce the idea that women's highest calling is to serve men, to be "good wives," to bear children, to prioritize family above their own personal ambitions. Every aspect of life has been engineered to keep women tethered to men, to make male companionship seem like an inevitability rather than a choice.

And yet, despite all of these carefully constructed barriers, women are leaving. The so-called dating crisis is not a crisis for women, it is a crisis for men who were promised a life in which women would never reject them. Women are no longer interested in playing the game when the rules are rigged, when the rewards are nonexistent, when the best possible outcome is settling for a man who sees them as an accessory rather than a partner. They are walking away from relationships that drain them, from marriages that exploit them, from social structures that demand their compliance while offering them nothing in return. And the industry of male entitlement is beginning to crumble under the weight of its own assumptions.

Men, recognizing this shift, are responding in the only way they know how, with panic, with coercion, with increasingly desperate attempts to legislate their way back into power. They push for policies that make it harder for women to access birth control and abortion, ensuring that an unwanted pregnancy can still be used as a tool to keep women financially and socially tied to men. They advocate for marriage incentives and tax benefits that pressure women into relationships they do not want. They whine about the death of traditional values, insisting that women's refusal to settle is an existential threat to society itself. And when those methods fail, they turn to outright punishment, removing legal protections, limiting divorce rights, pushing narratives that vilify independent women as selfish, bitter, or unnatural.

Because the truth is, they were never prepared for this. They never imagined a world where women had options, where marriage was not a survival necessity, where singlehood was not a tragedy but a liberation. They never considered that women might prefer to be alone rather than to be burdened with a man who expects everything and gives nothing. And now, faced with this new reality, they are floundering, grasping for solutions that will force women back into a system that no longer serves them.

But it will not work. Women have seen what life without male control looks like, and they are not going back. They have built alternative support systems, formed communities, secured their own financial independence. They have learned that they do not need men in their homes, in their lives, in their beds in order to be fulfilled. And the more they reject the industry of male entitlement, the clearer it becomes: this was never about companionship. It was about control. And now that women are choosing themselves, the entire foundation of male dominance is beginning to crack.

The Fragile Male Ego – The Tantrum When Women Say No

The fragile male ego cannot withstand rejection, not true, unmovable, unapologetic rejection. It can handle compromise, reluctant acceptance, a hesitant no that might eventually turn into a yes with enough pressure. But it cannot handle the kind of rejection that is absolute, the kind where women do not just refuse individual men, but the entire system designed to keep them compliant. The moment women say no, not just to marriage, not just to motherhood, but to male entitlement itself, the tantrum begins. It is loud, predictable, and utterly pathetic. It is the collective wailing of men who have been raised to believe they are owed access to women's time, labor, and bodies, and who are now being forced to reckon with the horrifying truth: they are not needed.

This is not a new phenomenon. The male tantrum has always been a part of history. It is the backlash that follows every moment when women attempt to claim their own autonomy. When women fought for the right to vote, men called it the end of civilization. When women fought for the right to work, they warned it would destroy the family. When women fought for the right to divorce, to control their own reproduction, to exist outside of marriage, the cries of outrage only grew louder. And now, as women make the final refusal, as they walk away entirely, as they reject relationships with men who bring nothing, as they decide that life is better without the burden of male entitlement, the reaction is even more desperate. Because this time, women are not just asking for inclusion. They are leaving men behind.

The tantrum plays out in predictable ways. The social whining begins first. Men take to podcasts, blogs, and social media to complain about how "modern women" are too entitled, too difficult, too demanding. They moan about how women no longer appreciate "good men," how feminism has made women impossible to satisfy, how it is unfair that they are expected to offer something in return for women's time and attention. They invent new language to describe their grievances, talking about how women are "hitting the wall," how they will "die alone," how feminism has tricked them into abandoning their "true nature." They rage about how society is collapsing because women will no longer settle, and they fantasize about a past where women had no choice but to tolerate them.

But when whining does not work, the threats begin. They turn to economic and legal punishment, demanding policies that coerce women back into dependence. They attack abortion rights, birth control access, no-fault divorce, any legal mechanism that allows women to control their own destinies. They push for tax penalties on single women, financial incentives for marriage, economic policies that make it harder for women to survive without a husband. They weaponize the courts against single mothers, fight to roll back workplace protections, try to make it impossible for women to walk away without suffering. Because when men realize they cannot make women want them, they attempt to make it impossible for women to function without them.

And when all else fails, when manipulation and coercion do not work, when women continue to reject them, the violence begins. The tantrum escalates into physical punishment, into mass shootings, into domestic terrorism fueled by male resentment. Women who reject men face the risk of stalking, harassment, and death threats. They are told they are unnatural, selfish, ungrateful, that they deserve whatever consequences come their way. And yet, men still believe they are the ones suffering. They convince themselves that they are the victims, that women refusing to tolerate them is somehow oppression, that their loneliness is something society must fix instead of something they brought upon themselves.

But the real crisis is not for women. Women are thriving without them. Women are forming communities, supporting each other, creating lives where men play no necessary role. Women are learning that they are happier, healthier, and freer when they are not burdened by male entitlement. And men, watching this unfold, are realizing too late that they were never the prize, never the indispensable force they believed themselves to be. They were placeholders, beneficiaries of a system that forced women to accept them. And now that women have choices, they are making different ones.

So the tantrum will continue. They will scream louder. They will try to legislate their way back into relevance. They will weaponize every tool they have left. But it will not work. Because women have already walked away. And once they are gone, they are never coming back.

The Economic and Social Independence That Scares Them

The economic and social independence of women has never been welcomed by those who have built their power on their subjugation. It has always been viewed as a threat, a disruption, a rebellion against the so-called natural order that men designed to serve themselves. They have spent centuries ensuring that women remained dependent, on marriage, on male wages, on a society that deemed them incomplete without the validation of a man. They created laws that barred women from owning property, from working, from earning their own money. They crafted social expectations that framed financial dependence as feminine virtue and submission as a necessity for survival. And now, as those structures collapse, as women break free from enforced reliance, men and the institutions that sustain them are panicking.

The entire foundation of patriarchy was built on one assumption: that women would always need men more than men needed women. It was not enough to convince women that they should want men, they had to ensure that women had no other option. This is why marriage was, for centuries, a legal contract where women lost all autonomy the moment they signed it. It is why financial independence was systematically denied to women, ensuring that even if a man was abusive, neglectful, or useless, she had no means of escape. It is why single women were socially and economically penalized, made to believe that without a husband, they would be left to suffer in poverty, loneliness, and disgrace.

But now, women are proving that none of it was ever true. They are earning their own money, buying their own homes, building their own businesses. They are creating networks of mutual support, investing in friendships, forming chosen families that do not revolve around men. They are realizing that men were never the security they were promised, that marriage was not a safety net but a trap, that every warning about what would happen to them if they rejected traditional roles was a lie. And nothing terrifies men more than this realization, that their presence in women's lives has been reduced to an option rather than a necessity.

It is no coincidence that the moment women started to secure financial and social independence, the backlash intensified. The laws began shifting, attacks on reproductive rights, attempts to restrict no-fault divorce, policies designed to push women back into economic vulnerability. The social narrative shifted, suddenly, single women were blamed for societal decline, warned about their ticking biological clocks, threatened with loneliness as if fear would be enough to undo their liberation. The financial system adjusted, wage gaps persisted, workplace discrimination remained, childcare and parental leave policies stagnated, all to make sure that independence came with obstacles. Because the more difficult it is for women to thrive on their own, the easier it is to pressure them into dependence.

But the truth is clear. Women do not need men. The myth of male indispensability is unraveling. And this is why they are panicking. They know that if women stop tolerating them, if women stop sacrificing for them, if women stop accepting the bare minimum as enough, men will have to offer something more. They will have to prove that they are worth inclusion in women's lives, that they bring more than just expectations, that they are not burdens demanding to be carried. And most of them will fail.

Because for centuries, men have never had to evolve. They have relied on a system that forced women to accept them no matter how little they contributed. They assumed that no matter how much women achieved, no matter how successful they became, they would always return to men, because they had been conditioned to believe that male approval was the ultimate validation. But that conditioning is breaking. Women are looking around, seeing their sisters thrive outside of marriage, seeing them live without the weight of a man dragging them down, and they are making different choices. And once that choice is made, there is no going back.

That is why the resistance to women's independence is so vicious. It is not about tradition. It is not about morality. It is about power. It is about a system that depends on women giving more than they receive, on women prioritizing men's needs over their own, on women believing that their survival depends on remaining within a structure that exploits them. And now that the structure is crumbling, men and the institutions that serve them will do everything in their power to restore it. They will make leaving harder. They will restrict access to abortion and birth control, force women into economic precarity, criminalize their autonomy if necessary. Because they know that if they cannot make women want them, they must ensure that women cannot afford to refuse them.

But they are too late. Women have already left. They have already begun building a new way of living, a new economy that does not revolve around men, a new social order where sisterhood replaces servitude, where women choose each other over the demands of a system that was never meant to serve them. They have already figured out that they were always the ones holding society together, always the ones keeping things running while men took credit, while men reaped the benefits of their labor without acknowledgment, without reciprocity, without gratitude. They have already realized that everything they were told about needing a husband, about fearing independence, about being incomplete without male validation, was a lie designed to keep them obedient, designed to trap them in a cycle of servitude masked as love, of unpaid labor disguised as duty.

They see now that their survival was never dependent on men, it was dependent on their ability to navigate a world that was structured against them, to endure, to work harder for less, to accept exhaustion as the cost of existence. And now, they refuse to accept it any longer. They refuse to shrink, to submit, to beg for what should have always been theirs. They refuse to participate in a system that demands their sacrifice but offers nothing in return.

And men, who have never had to exist outside of this system, are unprepared for what comes next. They are unprepared for a world where women do not automatically choose them, do not orbit them, do not shape their lives around male convenience. They are unprepared for a world where their role is no longer guaranteed, where their presence is no longer assumed to be a requirement for a woman's happiness, stability, or survival. They are unprepared to face the reality that without forced dependence, without economic and social coercion, without the manipulation of marriage and motherhood as inescapable destinies, they have nothing left to offer. They are unprepared to be unnecessary, to be unchosen, to be left standing on the sidelines of a world that is moving forward without them. And so, they rage, they threaten, they legislate, they scheme to force women back into dependence, back into fear, back into servitude. But none of it will work. Because once women taste freedom, they do not give it up. Once they see the lie for what it is, they do not fall for it again.

But their unpreparedness does not matter. The world is shifting, with or without them. The old order is dying, and no amount of tantrums, no amount of backlash, no amount of desperate attempts to claw back control will stop it. Women have stepped out of the roles they were once forced into, they have reclaimed their autonomy, they have built lives outside of the narrow expectations that were once suffocating them. And they are never looking back. The men who cannot evolve, who cannot accept a world where women are free, will be left behind, watching as the women they once took for granted, the women they assumed would always be there, disappear into a future where they are no longer needed.

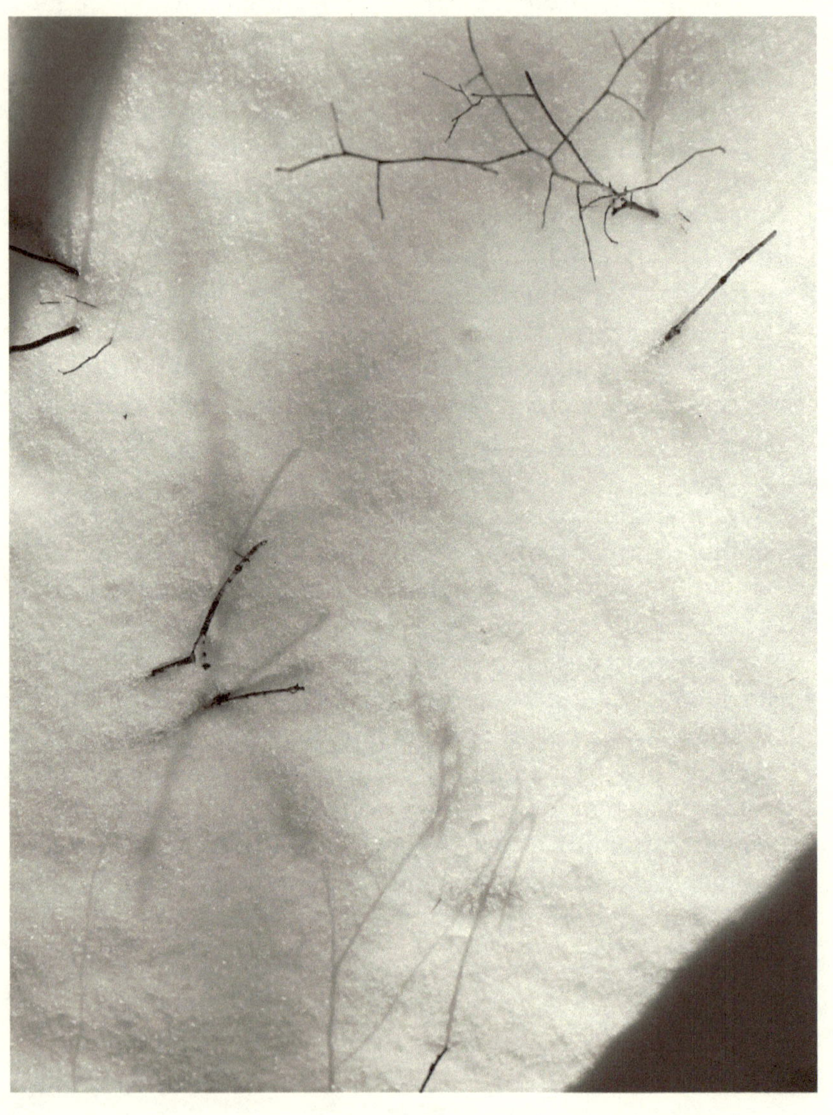

~3
The Cost of Dating is Too High
Dating is a Path to Forced Birth, Not Freedom

Dating is a path to forced birth, not freedom. They sold it to us as romance, as partnership, as the key to happiness, but in reality, it is nothing more than a well-disguised system of control. Every interaction with a man carries an unspoken risk, an unseen contract, a cost that is too high for women to keep paying. Because when a woman dates a man, she is not just entering a relationship, she is stepping into a structure designed to make her vulnerable, to wear her down, to keep her in a position where she can be controlled, whether through legal, economic, or biological means. And the most effective form of control, the one that has kept women tethered to men for millennia, is forced birth.

They tell us dating is about choice, but in a world where reproductive rights are under siege, what choice do we really have? The laws they are passing are not accidents, and they are not just about abortion. They are about eroding any form of autonomy that allows women to exist outside of male control. With abortion banned in over a dozen states and access being dismantled everywhere else, pregnancy is no longer just a medical condition, it is a potential life sentence. Birth control, which once gave women the ability to separate sex from reproduction, is next on their target list. Many states are already introducing legislation to restrict access to emergency contraception, IUDs, and even hormonal birth control. The trap is being set.

This is why dating is a risk that women can no longer afford. Because a single encounter, a single moment of trust, can cost a woman her entire future. It is not just about unwanted pregnancy, it is about the ability to escape. A woman who gets pregnant in the wrong state, with the wrong man, is no longer just a person. She becomes a ward of the state. She is trapped in a system that dictates what she can and cannot do with her body. She is forced into motherhood whether she wants it or not, her options systematically stripped away by men who will never face the consequences of their own laws.

And that is exactly how they want it. Because forced birth is not just about babies. It is about tying women to men in the most permanent way possible. It is about making sure she cannot walk away, making sure she remains dependent, making sure she has no other options. A pregnant woman is a woman whose freedom is in someone else's hands. A mother is a woman who is less likely to leave, less likely to fight back, less likely to demand more. They do not want partners. They want prisoners.

So they package dating as empowerment, as if it is something we should be grateful for, as if it is a privilege to navigate a system that increasingly resembles a minefield. And when women start realizing the cost is too high, when they start backing away, when they start refusing to play along, the backlash begins. Because if women are not dating, they are not at risk. If they are not in relationships, they are not trapped. If they are not sleeping with men, they are not getting pregnant. And if they are not having children, the entire structure of control begins to collapse.

This is why we are saying no. No more casual dating when casual dating comes with the risk of forced motherhood. No more relationships when relationships are just another avenue for control. No more pretending that this is about freedom when every policy, every law, every cultural expectation is designed to make sure we have none. If they want to turn pregnancy into a weapon, we will not give them the opportunity to use it. If they want to make dating a risk, we will choose not to take it. They think they can force us back into their system. They think they can scare us into compliance. They think they can trap us in a game we never agreed to play.

But we are walking away. And they are not ready for what happens when we do.

Men Expect Women to Fix Them, Teach Them, and Heal Them

Men expect women to fix them, teach them, and heal them. They have built an entire culture around this expectation, convinced that a woman's love, patience, and emotional labor are necessary ingredients for their growth and development. They enter relationships not as equals, but as projects, unfinished, emotionally stunted, often downright broken, fully expecting that the woman they date will put in the work to make them whole. They call it love. They call it partnership. But what they really mean is servitude.

From the moment a woman starts dating a man, she is expected to become his unpaid therapist, his life coach, his mother, his secretary. She is supposed to "understand" his failures, his shortcomings, his lack of communication skills. She is supposed to guide him through his emotional baggage, help him navigate his career, push him toward responsibility. If he is emotionally unavailable, she is expected to be patient. If he is immature, she is expected to teach him how to be an adult. If he has unresolved trauma, she is expected to nurture him through it. And the entire time, she is given the same promise, if she just invests enough, if she just gives enough, if she just proves herself worthy, he will eventually become the man she deserves.

But he never does. Because that was never the deal. The deal was that she would do the work, and he would reap the benefits. The deal was that she would mold herself around his needs while he remained exactly as he was, unchanged, unchallenged, unquestioned. She would compromise, sacrifice, lower her standards, accept less and less in exchange for the hope that one day, maybe, he would finally appreciate all she had done for him. And when he didn't? When he either left her for someone else or settled into complacency, never actually improving? It would still be her fault. She didn't try hard enough. She nagged too much. She expected too much. She was ungrateful, impossible to please.

This is how they keep women locked in a cycle of emotional exhaustion. This is why every woman knows what it feels like to be responsible for a man's feelings, why every woman has sat through an argument where she wasn't allowed to be upset because the man in front of her had made himself the victim. This is why women are told to be forgiving when men fail, to be understanding when men lash out, to be patient when men refuse to meet even the lowest expectations. Because the moment a woman demands more, the moment she stops making excuses, the moment she refuses to be a man's caretaker, the entire illusion falls apart.

And men know this. That is why they panic when women walk away. That is why they call independent women cold, bitter, damaged. That is why they insult single women, as if being alone is the worst fate imaginable, as if the alternative, being stuck in a relationship with a man who expects to be mothered, is somehow preferable. They rely on the idea that women will always return, always try again, always take on the work of fixing them, because that is how it has always been. They were never expected to develop emotional intelligence, to become responsible partners, to take care of themselves. Why would they, when every woman before us was told it was her job to do it for them?

But that cycle is breaking. Women are tired. Women are seeing the pattern for what it is. Women are realizing that dating is not about connection, or love, or mutual support, it is about work, and only one side is expected to do it. And when women choose not to? When they refuse to be therapists, teachers, and mothers to grown men? The men are left with nothing. No skills, no emotional depth, no ability to function in a relationship without being catered to.

And that, more than anything, is what they fear. Not just rejection, not just loneliness, but the realization that they never learned how to exist without a woman doing the work for them. And now, that work is over. We are done fixing them. We are done teaching them. We are done raising them. They can figure it out on their own, or they can be left behind. Either way, we are not wasting another second on their unfinished selves.

Refusing to Engage – How the Boycott Begins

Refusing to engage is how the boycott begins. Women have tried everything else, lowering their standards, giving men endless chances, explaining, negotiating, compromising. They have spent lifetimes tolerating immaturity, inconsistency, entitlement, and outright abuse, all while being told they are the problem. That they expect too much. That they should be more understanding, more forgiving, more patient. But the truth has always been clear: men expect everything and offer nothing. And now, women are realizing that the best response is not to argue, not to beg, not to wait for things to get better, but to walk away.

Because the cost of dating is too high. The risks are too great. A single bad decision, a single moment of misplaced trust, can derail a woman's life. Whether it is through an unwanted pregnancy, a financially draining relationship, an emotionally exhausting partnership, or an abusive dynamic that takes years to escape from, the reality remains the same: dating men is a gamble with overwhelmingly bad odds. And for what? A half-hearted text? A date she has to plan? A relationship where she is expected to be his mother, his maid, his life coach? A marriage that legally ties her to someone who will not lift a finger to make her life easier? The deal has never been worth it. It was just the only deal available.

But that is changing. Women are opting out. They are choosing friendships, careers, hobbies, independence, and self-respect over relationships that demand everything from them while giving nothing in return. They are refusing to waste time on men who refuse to grow, who believe that a woman's time is an infinite resource, who expect all the benefits of commitment while offering none of the security. They are leaving the dating pool, and in their absence, men are floundering.

And what do these men do in response? Do they reflect? Do they improve? Do they step up? No. They panic. They rage online, complaining about "modern women," about how feminism has ruined relationships, about how women "don't know their place" anymore. They demand that women lower their standards, return to traditional roles, accept them as they are. They don't ask what they need to do to be better. They don't consider that women are walking away because men have given them no reason to stay. They blame everyone but themselves.

That is why the boycott matters. Because no amount of explaining will change them. No amount of arguing will make them see the truth. The only way to make men understand their own irrelevance is to show them. To make them feel the absence of women's care, labor, time, and energy. To let them sit in the empty world they have created for themselves, where the only companionship they have is each other, angry, directionless, incapable of forming meaningful relationships because they were never taught to be worthy of them.

This is how we win. Not by fixing them, not by debating them, not by lowering ourselves to their expectations, but by leaving them behind. Let them deal with their loneliness. Let them figure out how to function without women propping them up. Let them feel, for the first time in history, what it means to not be catered to. Because they assumed we would always be there. They assumed we would always come back. They assumed we had no other choice.

They were wrong. We have a choice. And we are making it now. We are walking away. We are done explaining. We are done negotiating. We are done dating men. And we are never coming back.

Section 2
Do Not Have Sex with Men – Their Pleasure is Not Our Problem

~4
Abstinence, But Make It Revolutionary
How the Sex Strike Has Historically Created Change

The sex strike is not new. It is not radical. It is not extreme. It is one of the oldest and most effective forms of resistance women have ever used. Throughout history, when men have refused to listen, when they have refused to change, when they have doubled down on violence, oppression, and entitlement, women have done the one thing that forces them to pay attention: they have said no. Not just individually. Not just selectively. But collectively, as a strategy, as a movement, as a refusal to participate in a system that gives men power while forcing women to suffer.

The most famous historical example comes from Lysistrata, the ancient Greek play where women, sick of men's endless wars, organize a mass sex strike to force peace. It was satire, but it contained a deeper truth, men will only listen when they lose access to what they believe they are entitled to. And the sex strike is not just a fictional concept. Women have used it throughout history to demand change. In 2003, the women of Liberia, led by Leymah Gbowee, used a sex strike as part of their movement to end the country's brutal civil war. They refused sex with their husbands and lovers, making it clear that as long as men engaged in violence, they would not have access to women's bodies. And it worked. The movement helped force peace talks, leading to an end to the war and eventually to the election of Ellen Johnson Sirleaf, Africa's first female head of state.

There have been other sex strikes, too. In Kenya, women refused sex for a week in 2009 to pressure political leaders into working together. In Colombia, women launched the "crossed legs movement" to demand better infrastructure and an end to gang violence. In the Philippines, women withheld sex to force an end to deadly conflicts between warring factions. And in every case, the message was the same: as long as men refuse to build a world that is safe and just for women, they will not have access to women's bodies.

This is the power of refusal. The power of saying no, not just to one man, not just in one moment, but as a coordinated movement to strip men of the one thing they believe they are always owed. Because if history has shown us anything, it is that men do not change unless they are forced to. They do not reflect, they do not evolve, they do not question their entitlement unless they are made to suffer for it. And nothing makes men suffer more than losing sex.

This is why the idea of a sex strike is met with immediate hostility. The mere suggestion that women might collectively refuse sex is enough to send men into a panic, to make them rage, to make them mock, insult, and threaten. Because they know, deep down, that this is the one thing they cannot force without revealing who they truly are. They can pass laws that control our bodies. They can try to strip us of rights, force us into pregnancies, trap us in economic and legal dependence. But the one thing they cannot do, at least not without committing outright violence, is make us desire them. Make us want them. Make us come back.

And that is why they fear this movement. Because it exposes a truth they do not want to face: that without sex, without women's compliance, without women's willingness to participate in the system they have built, they have nothing. They are left alone, powerless, begging for the very thing they thought was their birthright. And the more women who refuse, the more men will be forced to realize that their pleasure is not our responsibility. That their entitlement is an illusion. That without our consent, they are nothing.

The sex strike is not just about punishment. It is about liberation. It is about breaking free from the idea that sex is something we owe, that relationships are something we must participate in, that our bodies exist to serve men's needs. It is about reminding them that we do not need them. That they need us. And that as long as they continue to treat us as objects, as second-class citizens, as things to be controlled rather than people to be respected, they will get nothing.

Because sex is not a right. It is not a given. It is not something men can demand or expect. It is something that must be earned. And right now, they have earned nothing.

Rape Culture is Built into Heterosexuality

Rape culture is built into heterosexuality. This is not an exaggeration. It is not an opinion. It is a fact. The way men are taught to pursue women, the way sex is framed in relationships, the way power dynamics are structured, it all normalizes coercion, minimizes consent, and places men's desires above women's autonomy. It is so embedded in the culture that many women do not even recognize it for what it is. We are taught from a young age that men push, and women are supposed to resist, just enough to make it interesting, but not so much that we are seen as cold or frigid. We are taught that a man being persistent is "romantic." That if he keeps asking, keeps pursuing, keeps trying, it means he really cares. That it is our job to say no the right way, to let them down gently, to avoid making them feel bad, to be careful not to provoke them. And if something happens that we did not want? We are expected to blame ourselves.

This is why so many women have had experiences they cannot fully name. Situations where they were pressured, where they were afraid to say no, where they did not want to but felt like they had to. Situations that left them feeling used, violated, or empty, but that they did not label as assault because, technically, they said yes. Technically, they agreed. But what they do not realize is that their agreement was never freely given. It was taken. Extracted through guilt, through pressure, through emotional manipulation. Women are taught to prioritize men's pleasure over their own boundaries. To be cool, to be chill, to be fun. To not be difficult, to not be selfish, to not be the girl who ruins the mood. This is rape culture. Not just in the extreme cases where men commit violent assaults, but in the everyday expectations that tell women they do not have the right to say no without consequence.

And when women begin saying no, collectively, the mask slips. The entitlement is exposed. We see it in the rage, the bitterness, the desperate attempts to shame and guilt women back into compliance. We see it in the men who say, "Fine, if you don't want to have sex, don't expect us to do anything for you." As if that was the deal all along. As if women were only ever valuable because they provided sex. As if the only reason men were ever willing to offer protection, provision, or even basic kindness was because they expected sex in return. When men respond this way, they are admitting that they never saw women as people in the first place. They saw us as a service, a commodity, something to be traded for favors, stability, and attention.

This is why a sex strike is so powerful. It forces the question: what happens when women no longer accept these terms? What happens when they refuse to participate in a system where sex is something they owe? What happens when women make it clear that they do not exist to satisfy men's desires, that their bodies are not rewards for good behavior, that their value is not tied to whether or not a man finds them useful? The answer is simple: men lose power. They lose their ability to manipulate, to control, to weaponize sex as a tool of compliance. They lose their ability to use relationships as a way to extract free labor. They lose the unearned privilege of being able to coast through life knowing that some woman, somewhere, will always be there to take care of them.

This is what terrifies them. Not just the lack of sex, but the loss of control. Because men who benefit from rape culture do not want enthusiastic, equal partners. They want women who are afraid to say no. They want women who feel pressured to say yes. They want a world where sex is something they expect rather than something they have to earn. And when that world starts to crumble, when women withdraw, when women refuse to participate, they will have nothing left but themselves, and that is the last thing they ever wanted to face.

What Happens When Women Say No—Collectively?

What happens when women say no, collectively? We are beginning to find out, and men are terrified. They always assumed we would never do it. That the idea of a mass sex strike was just a joke, an empty threat, something that could never truly happen because, in their minds, women need sex just as much as they do. They have convinced themselves that we crave them, that we depend on them, that we will never actually walk away. And now, as more and more women begin rejecting the idea that sex is something they owe, as more women opt out of relationships entirely, as more women openly say they are happier, healthier, and freer without men in their lives, the panic is setting in.

They cannot stand it. They mock the idea of a sex strike while simultaneously raging about how "modern women" are "ruining relationships." They belittle women who choose abstinence while also insisting that birth rates are declining and society is collapsing because women won't have enough babies. They say we are too picky, too high-maintenance, too demanding, yet they are the ones losing their minds at the realization that fewer and fewer women want to sleep with them. They want to have it both ways, they want to believe that they are superior, that women need them, that we are lost without them, while also throwing tantrums over the fact that women are doing just fine.

Because here is the truth: we do not need sex. They do. And they do not just need sex, they need women's participation. They need women to keep playing the game, to keep pretending that this is an equal exchange, to keep accepting less and less while giving more and more. They need women to be available, compliant, willing. They need us to believe that a life without men is a life unfulfilled because if we ever stop believing that, if we ever truly understand our own power, they lose everything.

And that is what is happening now. Women are seeing the truth. They are realizing that their lives are not diminished by the absence of men, but enriched by it. They are finding peace in being alone, joy in female friendships, fulfillment in careers and hobbies and passions that do not revolve around male approval. They are discovering that sex with men was never as good as men insisted it was, that the orgasm gap exists for a reason, that so much of heterosexuality was about performance, about catering to male pleasure, about fulfilling male fantasies while ignoring their own needs. They are learning that their value does not come from whether a man desires them, and that realization is breaking the system apart.

So what happens now? What happens when more and more women refuse? When they reject relationships, when they reject marriage, when they reject the idea that sex is something they owe or even want? What happens when men realize that their threats, their insults, their tantrums are doing nothing to stop the tide? What happens when women, collectively, simply walk away?

The answer is simple: men will have to evolve, or they will wither. They will have to learn how to be worth wanting, or they will be left behind. They will have to change, truly change, not just perform the bare minimum to get what they want. They will have to learn how to be emotionally intelligent, how to listen, how to give, how to be human in a way they have never been required to be before. Because if they do not, if they continue to expect women to carry all the weight, if they continue to believe they are owed access to women's bodies without effort, without respect, without genuine care, they will end up exactly where they belong, alone.

This is the future they created. They assumed we would never leave. But we are gone. And we are never coming back.

~5

The Rape Epidemic is a Policy Choice

The Legal Protection of Rapists in America

The legal protection of rapists in America is not an accident. It is not a loophole. It is not a failure of the system, it is the system. It is not a flaw in justice, not an unfortunate byproduct of bureaucracy, not a misalignment of legal processes. It is the very function of the state's machinery. The laws that govern sexual violence, the way cases are prosecuted, the way victims are treated, every piece of it is designed to protect men, not women. Every law passed, every policy enforced, every decision made by courts and law enforcement, carries with it the underlying assumption that women's suffering is inconsequential, that their violation is unfortunate but not intolerable, that rape is a regrettable event but not a crime worth dismantling institutions for. The entire structure exists to ensure that rapists remain free, that survivors remain silenced, that men can assault women with little to no consequence.

This is not new. The history of the legal system in the U.S. is a history of prioritizing men's rights over women's safety. For centuries, marital rape was not even considered a crime because a wife was legally the property of her husband. The legal definition of rape was never about the violation of a woman's body, it was about the violation of male property. A woman was raped if she was unmarried or if the rapist was not her husband. If she belonged to another man, if she was a daughter or a betrothed, then her assault was recognized as a crime, not against her, but against the man who claimed her.

Rape laws were written with the assumption that men were entitled to sex, that the only "real" rapes were those committed by strangers in dark alleys, and that anything else, especially if it happened within a marriage or relationship, was just a misunderstanding, a regrettable encounter, a moment of crossed signals. That foundation has never truly changed. It has evolved, it has been repackaged, but the core belief remains: protect the rapist, blame the victim, and let men continue as if nothing happened.

Look at the numbers. Fewer than 3% of rapists ever see a single day in jail. The vast majority never face charges at all. And the 3% who are convicted? They are given laughable sentences, released early, allowed to continue their lives while their victims live with the scars forever. Survivors are forced to relive their trauma, to have their credibility questioned, to be grilled about what they were wearing, what they drank, how many sexual partners they had.

Meanwhile, the men who commit these crimes are given every benefit of the doubt. Judges refuse to "ruin" their futures. Schools protect them to avoid bad press. Police departments fail to investigate because they know that even with overwhelming evidence, prosecutors are reluctant to take cases to court. The entire process is designed to discourage women from reporting, to remind them that the effort of seeking justice is more painful than the crime itself, that the only logical course of action is silence.

And it is not just the legal system that protects them. It is the entire cultural framework that surrounds rape in America. It is the way male celebrities, athletes, politicians, and CEOs are accused of sexual violence and face no real consequences. It is the way their defenders rally around them, calling their victims liars, gold-diggers, attention-seekers. It is the way the men who do get caught issue half-hearted apologies, do a short stint in PR rehab, and then return to their careers as if nothing ever happened. The machine of power ensures that rapists are not just protected, they are rehabilitated into society as if their crimes were minor errors, momentary lapses in judgment rather than acts of calculated violence. This is not about isolated incidents. This is a deliberate policy choice.

Because make no mistake: if they wanted to stop rape, they could. They could pass laws ensuring harsher penalties. They could fund sexual assault prevention programs. They could train law enforcement to take these cases seriously, eliminate the backlog of untested rape kits, make sure that serial offenders are held accountable before they have dozens of victims. They could create a system where a woman reporting an assault is believed, supported, protected. But they do not. Because stopping rape has never been the goal. Maintaining men's access to women's bodies without consequence has always been the priority. The criminal justice system does not fail women, it was never built to serve them. It was built to regulate their suffering, to quantify their pain, to determine which cases of violation were worth punishing and which could be ignored. It was built to preserve male dominance, to ensure that women could be used, discarded, and dismissed without disruption to the social order.

And that is why the rape epidemic is not just a crisis. It is policy. It is the result of deliberate decisions, upheld by lawmakers, enforced by courts, supported by a society that would rather let rapists walk free than create a world where women can exist without fear. They tell us that rape is a tragic but unavoidable reality, but that is a lie. It is not inevitable. It is allowed. It is sanctioned. It is woven into the very fabric of society, into the laws, into the courts, into the culture that teaches men they can take what they want and teaches women they must live with the consequences. And until women understand that, until we recognize that the system is not broken but working exactly as intended, we will continue fighting battles that were lost before they even began. The only solution is refusal. The only solution is rejection. The only solution is dismantling a world that was never built to protect us. Because we will never be safe in a system that exists to keep us vulnerable.

Why Good Men Must Prove Themselves, Not Just Declare It

Every time the rape epidemic is discussed, a chorus of men rushes forward with the same predictable response: *"Not all men."* They want to remind us that they personally have never raped anyone, that they would never harm a woman, that they are one of the good ones. They expect praise for meeting the absolute lowest standard of human decency, as if simply *not being a rapist* makes them special, as if it absolves them of any responsibility for the culture of male violence that they continue to benefit from. But here is the truth: if a man is truly good, he should not have to declare it. It should be obvious in his actions, in his choices, in his willingness to stand against the system that protects and enables rapists.

The problem with *"not all men"* is that it is a distraction. No one is accusing all men of being rapists, just as no one needs to be reminded that *some* men are decent. But the focus on individual innocence allows the collective guilt to go unchallenged. If every man insists that he is not part of the problem, then who, exactly, is responsible? If every man claims to respect women, then why is rape so widespread, why do laws continue to protect predators, why are sexual assault cases dismissed, why do men who hurt women continue to rise to the highest levels of power? If good men truly existed in the numbers they claim, rape culture would not exist. But it does. And that means too many of these so-called good men are doing absolutely nothing.

A man who stands silently while his friend harasses women is not a good man. A man who laughs at rape jokes but claims to be an ally is not a good man. A man who shrugs off sexual assault allegations against his favorite politician, actor, or sports hero because he does not want to *ruin their career* is not a good man. A man who watches his peers prey on younger women and does nothing is not a good man. A man who benefits from a world that makes women feel unsafe but refuses to challenge it is not a good man.

The men who insist *"not all men"* rarely follow up with *"but here is what I am doing to stop the ones who are."* They rarely examine their own complicity, rarely ask themselves if they have contributed to a culture that enables assault, rarely hold other men accountable in any meaningful way. They do not have to. Because the system does not require them to act. It allows them to be passive, to claim innocence without ever proving it, to move through life benefiting from the silence and inaction of other men who also call themselves good.

That is why it is not enough for men to simply *not* be rapists. They must be actively anti-rape. They must be willing to hold their friends, their coworkers, their brothers accountable. They must be willing to intervene, to challenge, to make other men uncomfortable. They must be willing to disrupt the status quo, to put themselves on the line, to risk their own social standing to ensure that women are not constantly left to fight this battle alone. Because if they are not willing to do that, then their goodness is not real. It is just another excuse to avoid responsibility.

Women do not need more men declaring themselves to be good. We need more men proving it. Because until they do, women will continue to assume that all men are dangerous, not because we believe they are, but because they have given us no reason to believe otherwise. Because as long as men refuse to challenge rape culture, as long as they continue benefiting from a world where women are forced to live in fear, as long as they remain silent when it matters most, their silence is complicity. And complicity is not goodness. It is cowardice. It is an active choice to uphold a system that allows rapists to walk free while survivors carry the burden of proof, of doubt, of shame. It is a declaration that their comfort, their ability to exist without confrontation, is worth more than women's right to live without fear.

Predators thrive in a world where sex is expected, where women are conditioned to be compliant, where men believe they are owed access to women's bodies. Rape culture does not just exist in dark alleys or back rooms, it is woven into the fabric of heterosexuality, into the way relationships are structured, into the belief that men pursue and women submit. It exists in the way women are pressured to be *nice,* to *give him a chance,* to *not make a scene.* It exists in the way women are told that if they say no too often, they will die alone. It exists in the way men are taught that their desires matter more than a woman's comfort, that if they push hard enough, wear her down enough, ignore her boundaries enough, she will eventually say yes.

This is why a sex strike is revolutionary. It is not just about withholding sex, it is about dismantling the conditions that allow sexual violence to flourish. It is about forcing men to confront a truth they have spent their entire lives avoiding: sex is not something they are owed. It is about disrupting the predator class, the men who prey on younger women, who take advantage of power imbalances, who use coercion and manipulation to extract consent from women who were never truly free to say no. Because when women start saying no, when they stop tolerating even the smallest forms of coercion, when they refuse to entertain men who expect access without effort, the entire system begins to fall apart.

This is why men panic at the idea of a sex strike. This is why they mock it, why they try to belittle it, why they insist that women are *only hurting themselves.* They know that sex has been their strongest form of leverage, their greatest tool of control. They know that if enough women refuse, if enough women walk away, they will be forced to evolve or be left behind. They know that without guaranteed access to women's bodies, without the ability to shame or pressure or manipulate their way into sex, they will be forced to develop something they have never had to develop before: actual worth.

Because right now, most of them have no worth. They do not bring anything to the table except expectation. They expect love without effort. They expect companionship without contribution. They expect sex without respect. They expect relationships without responsibility. And when women refuse? When they make it clear that they would rather be alone than settle? When they remove the automatic reward that men have been conditioned to believe they deserve? Men realize, too late, that they have nothing to offer.

And that is the point. To force a reckoning. To make men confront their own mediocrity. To make them realize that they cannot just *declare* themselves good, they must actually be good. That they cannot just *expect* sex, they must actually earn intimacy. That they cannot just *exist* and assume that women will accommodate them, they must actually contribute to a world where women feel safe, valued, respected.

If they cannot do that, they will be left behind. They will wither. They will be trapped in their own echo chambers, crying about *modern women,* about *feminism ruining everything,* about *why won't anyone sleep with me?* They will be stuck in their tantrums, watching as women move on without them, as women build lives where men play no role, as women realize that their worlds are better, safer, freer when they do not have to cater to male entitlement.

This is the future they created. They built a system where men could take without giving, where women were pressured into sex they did not want, where coercion was normalized and rape was excused. Now, women are taking back control. Now, women are saying no. And now, men must make a choice: evolve, or be forgotten. Because one thing is certain, we are never going back.

~6

Rewriting the Sexual Script

The Difference Between Liberation and Obligation

For too long, women have been told that sex is both their duty and their freedom. That their value is tied to their desirability, that their empowerment comes from being sexually available, that their worth is measured by how much they are wanted by men. It is a contradiction so deeply ingrained in society that many women do not even see it for what it is, a trap. We are told that withholding sex is oppression, that true liberation means embracing it, making ourselves open, accessible, eager. But at what point does *liberation* simply become another form of *obligation*? At what point does "sexual empowerment" just mean men getting unlimited access under a new name?

The sexual revolution was supposed to free women. It was supposed to give us control over our own bodies, to separate sex from shame, to allow us to engage on our own terms. And in many ways, it did. Birth control, abortion rights, the normalization of female pleasure, all of these things were wins. But men took that freedom and twisted it. They repackaged it as something that once again served them. They created a new expectation, one where women were still required to provide sex, but now under the illusion that it was our choice, that it was what we wanted, that it was what made us *strong, independent, and modern.*

But what happens when women realize they never actually wanted most of it? That they were participating in a system that never prioritized their pleasure, their comfort, their autonomy? What happens when they step back and question whether the *liberation* they were sold was just another method of coercion? Women were told that saying yes to everything was empowerment, but real empowerment is having the freedom to say no.

The truth is, most heterosexual encounters do not center women's pleasure. Studies consistently show the orgasm gap, where men reach climax far more often than women, is not biological, but cultural. Women are expected to perform sexuality, to act turned on, to make men feel desired, but their actual experiences are secondary. Men are taught that sex is something they take, not something they create with a partner. And because of this, most women have been conditioned to accept bad sex, uncomfortable sex, painful sex, sex they did not really want but felt obligated to provide. Sex as a chore, sex as a bargaining chip, sex as a means of keeping the peace in a relationship.

So what happens when we break the script? What happens when women stop treating sex as something they are supposed to give, and start treating it as something they only engage in when it is fully, enthusiastically, and completely for them? The answer is simple: men panic. Because for the first time, they realize how little they actually bring to the table.

If sex is no longer an obligation, if women are no longer performing desire for men's benefit, if they are no longer having sex out of guilt or pressure or fear of rejection, then men are forced to confront a reality they never wanted to face: most of them are terrible at sex, and without obligation, women would never sleep with them. They have built their entire world around the assumption that women will always be available, that women will always be eager to please, that women will always play along. But now, women are asking themselves a question they were never encouraged to ask: *Do I even want this?* And for many, the answer is no.

Because without the obligation, without the pressure, without the guilt, most men would never have sex at all. They have not put in the effort to be good lovers, to be attentive, to be generous, to be worthy of the kind of intimacy they demand. They have not done the work to be the kind of partners women genuinely crave. And now that women are recognizing that, men are starting to see the truth: they are not losing access to sex. They are losing access to sex they never deserved in the first place.

Why the Porn Industry Won't Survive Without Us

The porn industry is not just a business. It is not just entertainment. It is an institution built on the exploitation of women, the erasure of consent, and the industrialization of male entitlement. It exists to reinforce the idea that women's bodies are available, that sex is something to be taken rather than shared, that women exist for men's pleasure whether they want to or not. And without women's participation, without women playing along, believing that porn is *just fantasy,* believing that it has no real impact, the entire system collapses.

Men want to believe that porn is harmless, that it is just an outlet, that it has no bearing on how they treat women in real life. But we know better. We see the way porn rewires their expectations, the way it teaches them that sex is something they do to a woman, not with her. We see how it conditions them to expect instant compliance, no boundaries, no hesitation. We see the way it creates men who do not know how to have sex without domination, without aggression, without reducing their partners to objects.

And worst of all, we see how they bring those expectations into real life. We see the way teenage boys grow up watching violent, degrading porn and assume that is what sex is supposed to be. We see the way men expect real women to behave like the women they see in videos, silently compliant, endlessly willing, never saying no, never needing anything in return. We see the way men become completely detached from real intimacy, addicted to pixels on a screen, more aroused by fantasy than by the reality of a woman who has thoughts, feelings, needs, and limits.

This is why the porn industry is terrified of women waking up. Because the moment women realize that porn is not empowering, that it is not harmless, that it is not separate from the way men treat us, the entire structure falls apart. If women stop participating, if they stop normalizing it, stop defending it, stop allowing it to shape the way sex is discussed, men will be left alone in the world they created. They will be forced to confront what they have become, men who cannot function sexually without watching a woman be degraded. Men who cannot achieve arousal without imagining a woman's suffering. Men who have rewired their brains to crave control rather than connection.

And they do not want to face that. That is why they will fight so hard to convince women that porn is *just a fantasy*, that it is *not a big deal*, that *real men know the difference between porn and reality*. But we know better. We see the effects every day. We see it in the way men treat us, in the things they expect, in the way they react when women say no. We see it in the increasing number of men who cannot function in relationships because they are addicted to pornography, in the growing evidence that porn use destroys their ability to connect with real women.

And that is why porn will not survive if women stop playing along. Because without women normalizing it, without women accepting it, without women pretending it is just harmless fun, men will have to face what they have done to themselves. They will have to see how broken they are. How incapable they are of real intimacy. How much they have lost. And they will have no one to blame but themselves.

The only question left is this: will we continue allowing them to bring this sickness into our lives? Or will we walk away, let them rot in their porn-addled isolation, and force them to confront what they have become? Because without us, there is no industry. Without us, there is no normalization. Without us, they are just men alone in dark rooms, watching fake women on a screen, wondering why real women will no longer have them.

How to Deprogram Women from 'Service Mode'

Women have been conditioned to be in constant service mode, physically, emotionally, sexually. From a young age, we are taught that our role in relationships is to give, accommodate, nurture, and sacrifice. We are taught that men's needs come first, that our comfort is secondary, that sex is something we provide rather than something we experience. Even when women are told they are "equal" in relationships, the underlying expectation remains the same: women must work to keep men happy. This conditioning is not accidental; it is the backbone of a system that ensures men remain entitled while women are burdened with the emotional and physical labor of maintaining relationships. Women absorb the dysfunction, smooth out the rough edges, make things easier, while men grow accustomed to the luxury of being catered to without reciprocation. And if a woman refuses, she is labeled difficult, frigid, selfish, anything to shame her back into compliance.

This programming runs deep. It is why so many women fake orgasms, why they endure bad sex without complaint, why they convince themselves that sex is something they should want, even when they don't. It is why women lower their standards, make excuses for men who put in no effort, and stay in relationships where they are unfulfilled. It is why women feel guilty when they do not want sex, why they internalize the idea that their partner's frustration is their problem to solve, why they are constantly performing desire rather than experiencing it. The world has taught women to see their bodies as a product to be marketed, a prize to be won, a reward to be handed over in exchange for male approval. This is why so many women stay in relationships where they are neglected, dismissed, unsatisfied, because they have been told that their role is to make men happy, not to expect happiness themselves.

And it is all by design. Because the moment women step out of service mode, the moment they realize that they do not have to give men anything they do not want to give, the entire system collapses. The foundation of male entitlement crumbles when women stop believing that sex is something they owe, that relationships require sacrifice only from them, that love is synonymous with labor. A woman who understands that she can live without a man, that her worth is not tied to whether a man desires her, is a woman that patriarchy cannot control. And that terrifies them.

So how do we deprogram women from this role? How do we break the cycle of obligation, guilt, and self-sacrifice? The first step is understanding that desire is not the same as duty. Women have been raised to believe that sex is an obligation, that if they are in a relationship, they owe their partner intimacy. But sex that is given out of obligation is not sex, it is compliance. And compliance is not consent. Women need to unlearn the idea that their partner's satisfaction is their responsibility, that "keeping the relationship strong" means enduring intimacy they do not truly want. They need to understand that their body is not a tool for maintaining peace, for soothing egos, for keeping a man from straying. If sex is not desired, it should not happen, full stop.

The second step is recognizing that most men do not deserve what they demand. Women have been taught to give sex freely while asking for almost nothing in return. They have been conditioned to believe that their bodies are the reward, while men's presence alone is the prize. But why? Why do so many women accept sex that does nothing for them? Why do so many endure partners who do not care about their pleasure, who make no effort to learn their bodies, who expect unlimited access while putting in no work? The answer is simple: because they were told that expecting more would drive men away. And for generations, women feared that. They feared loneliness more than they feared a lifetime of unsatisfying sex, emotional neglect, and being treated as an afterthought. But what if we let them go? What if we stopped clinging to men who do not meet even the bare minimum? What if we stopped treating their orgasm as an achievement, their attraction as validation, their approval as something we should strive for? What if we refused to engage in intimacy that did not bring us pleasure?

The answer is clear: most men would never have sex again. And that is exactly what needs to happen. Because until men learn that women are not service providers, until they realize that sex is supposed to be mutual, that their partner's pleasure is not secondary to their own, they do not deserve access to women at all. Men do not deserve intimacy simply for existing, for being in the room, for being available. If they cannot offer more than a body that takes without giving, then they should receive nothing. The imbalance exists only because women continue to tolerate it, to excuse it, to participate in it even when it does not serve them. But the moment women decide they are done, the moment they collectively refuse to keep lowering the bar, men will be forced to evolve, or be left with nothing.

The final step is teaching women that walking away is power. The moment a woman understands that her life is better without men who drain her, who take without giving, who expect without earning, she is free. She is free from faking, free from enduring, free from guilt, free from the lie that sex is something she must provide rather than something she chooses to engage in. She is free from men who believe that her worth is tied to their pleasure. She is free from the burden of managing men's emotions, soothing their insecurities, making them feel strong, making them feel wanted. And in that freedom, she realizes the truth, they need us. We do not need them. And without us, they have nothing.

Section 3
Do Not Marry Men – The Ultimate Trap

~7

The Myth of the Good Husband

Marriage as a Patriarchal Scam

Marriage has always been an institution of domination, a contract not of love but of ownership, designed to ensure that men possess, consume, and extract from women without reciprocation. It has never been a mutual agreement between equals, but a structure that binds women to the service of men, to the labor of maintaining their homes, raising their children, soothing their egos, and absorbing the violence of their failures. It is a system built to guarantee male ease at the expense of female exhaustion, to institutionalize women's subjugation under the guise of stability. And yet, for centuries, women have been conditioned to believe that this is the highest aspiration, that marriage is security, that a good husband is the ultimate prize. But security from what? Protection from whom? A prize for whom? It has always been a lie, a fabrication meant to trap women into unpaid labor, into reproductive servitude, into financial dependence that makes leaving nearly impossible.

And yet, women have clung to the fantasy that the right man will undo the structure itself, that a loving, progressive husband will shield them from the inherent inequality of marriage. But the truth is that marriage is not merely about individual men. It is an institution designed to extract from women and give to men, regardless of intent. A man does not have to be cruel to benefit from this system; he only has to exist within it. The very design of marriage ensures that the woman will always give more, will always carry the heavier burden, will always be expected to sacrifice while the man receives. Even the most "equal" of marriages eventually settle into the same well-worn pattern: she becomes the manager of the household, the primary caregiver of the children, the social planner, the emotional regulator, while he is praised for participating in the barest minimum of domestic life. Society will call him a "good husband" if he does the dishes once a week, if he "helps" with the baby, if he expresses any emotion beyond entitlement and withdrawal. Meanwhile, she will be judged, criticized, and blamed for everything that goes wrong, whether it is the state of the home, the health of the relationship, or the emotional well-being of the children.

This is not an accident. This is how marriage was built to function. Women enter into it full of optimism, believing that they will be the exception, that they will be able to negotiate an equal partnership. But the weight of centuries is against them. The moment a woman says, "I do," she steps into a role that was crafted for her long before she was born, and that role is not one of freedom, but of obligation. And if she dares to question it, if she begins to realize that she is exhausted, unfulfilled, burdened beyond measure, the response is always the same: try harder. Communicate better. Be more patient. Lower your expectations. Marriage does not adjust to accommodate women's needs, women are expected to adjust themselves to accommodate marriage.

But the system is breaking. Women are walking away, not just from individual marriages, but from marriage itself. They are recognizing that they were never the beneficiaries of this arrangement, only the servants of it. The numbers speak for themselves: marriage rates are falling, divorce rates are rising, and fewer women are willing to enter into a contract that has never served them. And the panic is palpable. Men are scrambling to reclaim their lost control, lawmakers are rolling back reproductive rights, religious leaders are issuing frantic warnings about the decline of "family values." They are not concerned with women's well-being, they are concerned with maintaining the system that kept women bound to them for generations. Because marriage was never about love. It was about ensuring that men had access to free labor, to free childcare, to bodies they could use and discard, to emotional support without accountability. And now, faced with the reality that women are choosing themselves, that they are opting out of servitude, men are forced to confront their greatest fear: irrelevance.

Because the truth has always been that men needed marriage, not women. They needed wives to anchor them, to care for them, to structure their lives, to give them purpose where they had none. Women, on the other hand, are discovering that they are not just capable of surviving without husbands, they are thriving. Single women are wealthier, healthier, happier. They are building lives centered around their own desires, their own ambitions, their own freedom. They are rejecting the notion that they must tie themselves to men to be whole, rejecting the idea that security comes from a contract that benefits only one side.

And so, marriage is unraveling, not because women have changed, but because they have finally seen the truth. The illusion is shattered. They no longer need to be convinced that marriage is a trap. They know. And once that knowledge spreads, there is no turning back. Marriage is not a partnership. It is a structure of control. And now, at last, women are walking away from it, never to return.

The Legal System Exists to Control Wives, Not Help Them

Women are told that marriage offers them security. That it is a protection, a safety net, a promise that they will be cared for. But protection from what? Security from whom? The reality is that marriage is not designed to protect women, it is designed to control them. From the moment a woman signs a marriage certificate, she is entering a legal contract that prioritizes her husband's rights over her own. It has always been this way. It was true when women were considered the legal property of their husbands, when they could not own land or have their own bank accounts, when they could not sign contracts or make medical decisions without their husband's permission. And even though women today are told they have equal legal standing in marriage, the remnants of that system still remain. The structure of marriage still assumes that men are the default, that women are the dependents, that a wife exists to support, serve, and endure.

Divorce laws still overwhelmingly favor men. Courts still assume that children belong with the father if he decides to fight for them, no matter how uninvolved he was before the split. Alimony and child support are constantly under attack, framed as "unfair" to men who would rather see their ex-wives struggle than take financial responsibility. Women who leave their marriages are still more likely to experience financial instability, especially if they took on more unpaid labor during the relationship, which most wives do. Women scale back their careers, take on more household duties, do the work of parenting while their husbands claim the title of "provider." But when the marriage ends, women are left scrambling to regain financial footing while men, statistically, see their wealth increase.

Meanwhile, men benefit from marriage even after it ends. They come out of divorce wealthier, more likely to remarry, and often with no meaningful consequences for whatever damage they caused. They do not have to worry about losing custody of their children. They do not have to rebuild their lives from scratch. They simply move on, while their ex-wives struggle to recover from the years of sacrifice they were expected to make.

And for women who stay? The legal system ensures that their options are limited. Marital rape is still legal in some states, and even in places where it is technically outlawed, it is rarely prosecuted. Abused women are often trapped by financial dependence, by custody laws that threaten to give their children to their abuser, by police and courts that minimize domestic violence and turn a blind eye to the ways men use the legal system to further control their wives. And if a woman manages to leave, the danger does not end, the most dangerous time in an abusive relationship is when a woman tries to escape. Women are murdered by their husbands and ex-husbands every day, because for many men, the moment a woman decides she no longer belongs to him, she becomes disposable. The very institution that is supposed to protect women places them in more danger, and still, they are told they must endure, they must try harder, they must hold the family together.

This is the reality of marriage. It is not a fairytale. It is not a partnership. It is a legal structure designed to trap women in relationships they may not be able to leave, with men who are conditioned to take more and give less. It does not matter if he is kind, if he "isn't like other men," if he "believes in equality." He still benefits from a system that treats wives as second-class, as supporting characters in their husband's story. Every tradition, every law, every social expectation around marriage is built to keep women bound, to make leaving difficult, to enforce the idea that a woman's purpose is to stay, to endure, to accept whatever she is given. And when women try to fight back, they are punished. Single women are demonized, divorced women are blamed, child-free women are shamed. Every possible outcome outside of marriage is framed as failure, as loneliness, as a tragedy. Because men know that if women stop believing in marriage, if they stop seeing it as their best option, the entire system collapses.

And this is why women are starting to walk away. Because once you see it, once you understand that marriage is not a contract of love but a contract of control, there is no way to unsee it. And there is no reason to sign up for it. A future without marriage is not just possible, it is necessary. And the more women realize this, the faster the world changes.

Men have always needed women more than women have needed men. This is the fundamental truth that patriarchy has spent centuries trying to obscure. Every structure of male power, from marriage to religion to economic dependence, was designed not because men were stronger or more capable, but because they knew that without women's labor, without women's time, without women's willingness to endure, they would collapse. And now, the foundation of that power is beginning to crack. The boycott is not simply about rejecting individual men. It is about dismantling the entire system that has made women believe that men are necessary, that they must always be accommodated, that they will inevitably be part of women's futures. But what if they are not? What if they have outlived their usefulness?

For too long, women have been burdened with the responsibility of guiding men toward decency. They have been expected to mold them, to tolerate their stunted emotional development, to patiently teach them how to be human. They have absorbed men's failures, excused their shortcomings, and allowed them to remain perpetual children, incapable of standing on their own without a woman propping them up. But no more. The boycott is not an argument. It is not a campaign to convince men to do better. It is an abandonment of the idea that men are entitled to women's energy simply because they exist. And without women to soften the world for them, without women to clean up their messes, to bear their children, to absorb their rage and their disappointments, men will finally be forced to confront themselves.

And what will they find? A generation of men who never learned to build real relationships, who were told their mere presence was enough, who were never asked to do more than the absolute minimum. A generation of men who, for the first time, will have to experience rejection not as an anomaly, but as the default. For centuries, women have been told they must make themselves desirable. They must diet, must groom, must smile, must make themselves small enough, quiet enough, pleasant enough to be chosen. But men? They have simply existed, assured that no matter how little they bring to the table, there will always be a woman willing to take them in. That illusion is crumbling.

As more women walk away, refuse to marry, refuse to mother, refuse to be free labor for men who offer nothing in return, the panic will grow. They will rage, they will threaten, they will attempt to legislate their way back into power, but none of it will work. Because women have finally learned the one truth that men have feared all along: life without men is not just possible, it is better. Women without husbands live longer, are wealthier, have less stress, and more freedom. Women without male partners build deeper friendships, create alternative family structures, and thrive in ways patriarchy has worked tirelessly to suppress. Men have spent centuries convincing women that a world without them is unthinkable, but the moment women start thinking it, imagining it, living it, the entire system begins to break.

The boycott is not about fairness. It is not about giving men the chance to catch up. It is about declaring, finally, that the burden of change is no longer on women. If men want to be part of the future, they will have to prove they deserve it. They will have to rebuild themselves from the ground up, without expecting women to hold their hands, to do the work for them. And if they refuse? If they continue to flail and tantrum and blame women for their irrelevance? Then they will find themselves exactly where they deserve to be, alone, obsolete, left behind. Because women are not waiting. Women are not begging. Women are not slowing down. The world they are building is one where men are no longer needed, no longer default, no longer the center of gravity. The only question that remains is whether men are capable of meeting the standards that women have long surpassed.

~8
The State Uses Marriage to Enforce Women's Submission

Forced Birth and Forced Marriage are Part of the Same System

Forced birth and forced marriage are part of the same system. They are two arms of the same machine designed to control women, to limit their options, to ensure that they remain dependent on men and the state. It is no coincidence that the same lawmakers pushing for abortion bans are also advocating for policies that make it harder for women to leave marriages. The goal is not just to restrict reproductive rights, it is to strip women of autonomy entirely. A woman who cannot control whether or not she becomes a mother is a woman who cannot control the course of her own life. A woman who is tied to an unwanted child is more vulnerable, more economically dependent, more easily coerced into a marriage or a relationship she would have otherwise avoided. And that is exactly the point. Forced birth is not about the sanctity of life. It is about ensuring that women remain bound to men, legally and financially, trapped in a cycle of dependency.

When a woman loses the right to control her body, she loses the ability to control her future. If she cannot access birth control, if she cannot terminate a pregnancy, if she is forced to carry an unwanted child, her economic and social freedom disappears. The more children she has, the more tied she becomes to the men in her life. This is why forced birth is not just about babies, it is about forcing women into marriages they do not want and lives they cannot escape. A woman burdened with multiple children, with no access to abortion or reproductive healthcare, faces few choices. She is less likely to leave an abusive partner. She is less likely to pursue higher education or a career. She is more likely to become financially dependent on a man who will never see her as an equal, only as a caregiver, a servant, a body for his use.

And the state makes sure that once a woman is married, leaving is as difficult as possible. Divorce laws, custody battles, financial penalties, all of these barriers exist to ensure that even if a woman realizes she made a mistake, she has no easy way out. In many states, custody laws still favor fathers, regardless of their history of abuse or neglect. Financial settlements often leave women worse off than the men they are divorcing. And social stigma reinforces the idea that a woman who leaves her marriage has failed, even when staying would have meant enduring misery or violence. The state reinforces male power by making sure that women who leave their marriages face economic hardship, social ostracization, and legal obstacles. Women who stay, even in bad marriages, are told it is for the good of the family, for the good of the children, for the stability of society. And women who try to escape often find themselves facing not just an angry ex-husband, but a system that protects him at every turn.

This is not accidental. It is a deliberate strategy to keep women trapped. Because when women are free to walk away, when they are not bound by forced birth, forced dependency, or legal barriers, men lose control. And the state, run by those same men, will do everything it can to make sure that does not happen. This is why abortion rights and marriage laws are always legislated hand in hand. The same politicians who want to ban abortion are the ones gutting social welfare programs, making childcare unaffordable, restricting access to divorce. The goal is not to help women raise children. It is to force them into circumstances where they cannot leave. It is to ensure that they remain tied to men, regardless of whether those men are good partners, good fathers, or even safe to be around.

Historically, marriage was never a contract between equals. It was a transfer of ownership, a way to ensure that women belonged to men legally and socially. In some cultures, a woman moving from her father's house to her husband's was literally described as a change in guardianship, as if she were property being passed along. That legacy still lingers in modern marriage, no matter how much society pretends otherwise. The last names we inherit, the tax benefits we distribute, the legal framework that still assumes men are the head of the household, all of it reinforces a hierarchy where women are expected to submit. And now, as more women refuse to participate in marriage, as they reject the institution that was designed to limit them, the backlash has been immediate.

When women start rejecting marriage? When they refuse to participate in a system designed to control them? The alarm bells start ringing. Politicians sound the alarm about falling birth rates. Religious leaders insist that society is collapsing because women refuse to be wives. Right-wing think tanks scramble to find new ways to push women back into the role of obedient, unpaid caregivers. And men, realizing that their access to sex, domestic labor, and free emotional support is being cut off, begin to panic. They never had to build lives without women carrying them. They never had to function without a wife smoothing out their failures. And now that women are walking away, they are scrambling to rewrite the rules to force them back in.

But the more they tighten their grip, the more women resist. The more they try to force women into marriage, the more women refuse. The more they criminalize abortion, the more women refuse to have sex, refuse to engage, refuse to give men the children they so desperately need to maintain their power. The state can pass all the laws it wants. It can strip away rights, punish women for being independent, attempt to legislate us back into submission. But it cannot force us to participate. It cannot make us marry men who do not serve us. It cannot make us birth the next generation of oppressors.

And that is why they are afraid. Because they are realizing, too late, that without our compliance, their system crumbles. And women, for the first time, are refusing to comply.

The Lie of Male 'Breadwinners' – Most Men Provide Nothing

The myth of the male breadwinner is one of the greatest scams ever sold to women. It is the foundation upon which marriage has been justified for centuries, the idea that men are providers, that they offer financial security, that women benefit from being tied to a husband who will take care of them. This lie has been repeated so often, with such confidence, that even modern women still believe it. They still hear the echoes of past generations warning them that they need a man, that without one, they will struggle, that marriage is a necessity, not a choice. They have been conditioned to believe that men are the ones who build homes, who secure the future, who make life easier.

But the numbers, the reality, the daily experience of women proves the opposite. Most men provide nothing. Most men take more than they give. And the ones who do provide financially rarely offer anything else, no emotional labor, no domestic contributions, no true partnership. They simply exist, expecting to be served, expecting their presence alone to be enough. The numbers prove it. In modern marriages, women contribute just as much, if not more, financially than their husbands. Women work full-time jobs, and yet they are still expected to handle the majority of household labor, childcare, and emotional management. The so-called provider is often just another dependent, another obligation, another weight that drags her down.

Even in cases where a man earns slightly more, the difference is often negligible, and in many cases, it comes at the direct expense of the woman's career, because she is expected to sacrifice her ambitions, scale back her hours, or take on unpaid domestic responsibilities to support his success. Women are pushed into lower-paying fields, into part-time work, into schedules that allow them to be the primary caregivers while men's careers flourish. And when women dare to prioritize their own ambitions, when they refuse to sacrifice for a man's advancement, they are accused of being selfish, of failing as wives, of not doing their part. The entire system is rigged to ensure that men benefit, no matter how little they contribute.

And when we look at single women? The lie falls apart completely. Study after study shows that single women are financially better off than married women. They save more, they invest more, they have more financial independence. The economic penalty for being a wife is real. Once married, women statistically end up with fewer assets, lower earnings, and more financial risk, especially if they have children. Meanwhile, single men are worse off than married men. They are less stable, less healthy, more likely to struggle financially. Why? Because marriage benefits men at the expense of women. It is not an equal partnership, it is a wealth transfer, where women give and men take.

And let's talk about the men who make no effort at all. How many women have found themselves in marriages where they are not just equal earners, but the primary or only breadwinner? How many women have husbands who refuse to work, who contribute nothing, who sit at home playing video games, making excuses, treating their wives like built-in caretakers rather than partners? How many women marry men believing they will be providers, only to find themselves supporting a grown child in a man's body?

These men are not rare. They are everywhere. They exist in marriages where the wife is exhausted, overworked, and financially strained while the husband drifts through life, believing that his mere presence is enough to justify his place in the household. They exist in homes where the woman does everything, earns the paycheck, cleans the house, raises the children, while the man barely contributes and yet still expects respect, still demands submission, still insists that he is the head of the household.

Because here is the reality: marriage is not about men providing for women. It is about men securing lifelong caretakers, free domestic labor, a built-in emotional support system, and a financial safety net. Men do not get married to provide. They get married to be taken care of. And when women realize this, when they start doing the math, when they see that their lives would be easier, richer, freer without a husband dragging them down, men panic.

This is why they push the idea that women must marry. Why they shame women who remain single. Why they insist that men are the foundation of society, even though it is women who hold everything together. Because the second women start questioning the breadwinner myth, the second they ask what, exactly, men are bringing to the table, the second they stop blindly accepting the idea that they need a husband to survive, the entire structure crumbles. And that is exactly what is happening.

Women are waking up. Women are leaving marriages, avoiding them altogether, building their own wealth, their own communities, their own stability without men. They are realizing that the promises of marriage were never about their benefit, that the entire institution was designed to extract from them, to keep them in service to men who were never required to offer anything in return. And now, men, for the first time, are realizing that they have no idea how to function without women carrying them.

They spent generations telling us we needed them. But now, they are the ones who are lost without us.

Marriage has never been about partnership. It has never been about love, equality, or shared responsibility. It has always been a trap, carefully designed to bind women to men in ways that make leaving nearly impossible. It is a system built to ensure that even when a woman realizes she wants out, the cost, financially, legally, socially, is so high that she hesitates. That she stays. That she endures. Because marriage is not structured to benefit both people equally, it is structured to lock women in. A contract masquerading as romance, a lifelong commitment engineered to secure male convenience at the expense of female autonomy. Women are told that marriage is the pinnacle of life's purpose, the thing that will complete them, secure them, give them protection in old age.

But this was always a lie. Marriage does not protect women. It does not enrich them. It drains them. It traps them in a cycle of unpaid labor, of emotional exhaustion, of financial dependence. It is a system built for men's benefit, upheld by legal, cultural, and social structures that all point toward one goal: ensuring that women never realize they were always better off alone.

From the moment a woman marries, her autonomy shrinks. Even if she keeps her last name, even if she insists on maintaining financial independence, the weight of cultural and legal expectations immediately shifts onto her shoulders. She is now responsible for the home, for the emotional labor, for ensuring the relationship functions smoothly. The man, even if he enters the marriage promising to be an equal partner, gradually defaults to the role that society has carved out for him, the one who gets to do less. He will be praised for doing the bare minimum. He will be celebrated for "helping" around the house. He will not be expected to notice what needs to be done, to carry the mental load, to manage the relentless, invisible labor that keeps a household functioning. And when he inevitably fails to meet even the most basic expectations, the response is never to hold him accountable. Instead, the woman is told to "work on the relationship," to "communicate better," to "be more understanding."

This is not coincidence. It is how marriage was built to function. Historically, marriage was nothing more than a contract of ownership. A woman was transferred from her father's house to her husband's, legally becoming his property. Her labor, her body, her ability to bear children, all of it was included in the deal. Even today, the echoes of this remain. The expectation that a wife will take her husband's last name. The wedding tradition of a father "giving away" his daughter. The legal and financial incentives that encourage women to merge everything with their spouse, making separation exponentially harder. And the moment she steps into this role, the world reinforces that her purpose is now service. If she thrives, it is expected. If she suffers, it is her failure. The system ensures that even the most independent, strong-willed woman will find herself drained, exhausted, worn down by the relentless expectations placed upon her.

And if a woman wants to leave? She pays the price. Divorce is designed to punish women. Even in cases where the husband is abusive, even in cases where the marriage has long been dead, women face more financial hardship, more social stigma, and more personal risk than their male counterparts. Divorce court is not built to protect women, it is built to make them regret leaving. Custody battles favor men who weaponize the legal system to punish their ex-wives. Courts still operate under the assumption that women should be primary caregivers but do not offer the financial protections that should come with that role. Many women, even those who are financially independent, still find themselves economically devastated after a divorce, while men often recover quickly, free to start over with little to no long-term impact. And for those who stay, believing they are in equal partnerships? The data tells the real story.

Married women are less happy, more stressed, and take on more unpaid labor than their husbands, even when they work full-time jobs. Studies show that women who avoid marriage live longer, save more money, and experience less overall stress. The supposed benefits of marriage are a myth, a carefully constructed illusion meant to keep women locked in. The reality is clear: marriage does not improve women's lives. It burdens them. It extracts from them. It takes more than it gives. And yet, despite all of this, women are still encouraged to believe that their best option, their highest aspiration, is to be a wife. Why? Who benefits from this lie? Not women.

Women are still sold the idea that marriage is security, that without a husband, they will be alone, vulnerable, incomplete. But the truth is, marriage was never about women needing men. It was always about men needing women. Men need the unpaid labor, the emotional support, the financial sacrifices. They need the structure that ensures there will always be a woman cleaning up after them, making their meals, managing their homes, tending to their children. And the more women who refuse to engage, the more obvious it becomes: men are scrambling. Because for the first time in history, women are seeing marriage for what it is, not a necessity, not a protection, not a dream, but a structure built to secure male comfort at the expense of female autonomy.

And as more women walk away, as they reject marriage, as they build lives that do not revolve around men, they are proving something men never wanted to acknowledge: that women were always the ones holding everything together. That women never needed husbands, husbands needed them. And now, they are the ones left scrambling, watching as the foundation of marriage crumbles, powerless to stop what was always inevitable.

~ 9

The Alternative to Marriage – Radical Sisterhood

Building Community Without Men

For generations, women were taught that their survival depended on marriage. That without a husband, they would be alone, vulnerable, struggling to get by. That a woman without a man was a failure, a tragedy, a cautionary tale. But this was never true. It was only the story they told us to keep us dependent. Because the truth is, women do not need men to survive. Women need each other. The idea that women must attach themselves to men for protection, for financial security, for companionship, was never a reality, it was a narrative designed to keep women afraid, to make them believe that their only path to stability was through service to a man. But history tells a different story.

Long before the nuclear family, before men consolidated power into laws that forced women into economic dependence, women survived through communal bonds, through sisterhood, through structures that did not require male approval or control. Women have always built networks of care, have always raised children together, have always protected one another when men abandoned them, failed them, or turned violent against them. The only thing that changed was the world men built, a world that deliberately isolated women, cut them off from one another, and forced them into marriage not as a choice, but as a means of survival.

Marriage was never the only way to build security. Women have always created alternative forms of family, sisterhood, and communal living to protect themselves when men failed to provide. Before capitalism isolated women into nuclear households, before the modern economy forced women into financial dependence on men, women lived together, raised children together, worked together, and survived together. Women thrived in multi-generational homes, in networks where they could rely on one another, in systems that were not designed to make them the sole caretakers of men who refused to do the same in return. The idea that a woman alone must struggle is a manufactured lie, one designed to keep women afraid of choosing independence, of choosing themselves. And yet, as more women reject marriage, as they refuse to build their lives around men, we are already seeing the return of radical sisterhood.

More women are choosing to live together, pool resources, and create lives that do not revolve around men. They are buying homes together, co-parenting, sharing childcare responsibilities, and prioritizing friendships over romantic relationships. They are rejecting the notion that a single romantic partner must be the foundation of their life, that a man must be the center of their happiness, that marriage is the only path to stability. They are realizing that the strongest, most fulfilling, most reliable relationships in their lives have never been with men, they have been with other women. And as they invest more in these relationships, as they shift their attention away from marriage and into building communities that actually support them, men are left scrambling to figure out where they fit.

The power of women-centered communities is that they are built on reciprocity rather than extraction. Unlike marriage, where men take and women give, sisterhood is about mutual support. Women who form communities outside of marriage are not bound by legal contracts or patriarchal expectations. They are bound by real connection, shared goals, and the understanding that they do not need to serve men to live meaningful lives. And this is why men panic when women stop marrying. It is why they try to shame single women, why they mock friendship, why they demean any structure that does not center them. Because they know that once women realize they can build security without husbands, the entire marriage economy collapses. They know that if women stop believing that they need men, they will never again settle for the miserable half-existence that men have offered.

So what does a world without marriage look like? It looks like women thriving. It looks like houses filled with love and laughter, where no one is exhausted from carrying the weight of an incompetent, emotionally unavailable husband. It looks like financial stability without the burden of supporting a man who refuses to contribute. It looks like women choosing companionship without pressure, relationships without coercion, intimacy without obligation. It looks like women making decisions about their futures without worrying how a man will react, how he will feel, how much of herself she will have to give up to make him comfortable. It looks like women building lives where they are not second to anyone, where their needs come first, where they are not told that they must settle, endure, tolerate, and sacrifice in order to be worthy of love.

And most of all, it looks like freedom. Freedom from the constant labor of managing a man's emotions. Freedom from the invisible load of unpaid work. Freedom from the fear of being abandoned after years of sacrifice. Freedom to live, to dream, to build, to create a life that is truly our own. This is not a fantasy. It is already happening. Women are already walking away, already forming new structures, already proving that life outside of marriage is not just possible, it is better. And as more women step into this reality, the myth of marriage as a necessity will finally die. Because the truth has been revealed. Women do not need husbands. They never did. And now, they will never have to pretend otherwise again.

For too long, women have been made to believe that marriage is survival. That without a husband, they would struggle financially, live in loneliness, and have no one to support them in old age. This lie has been reinforced by generations of economic policies that made it harder for women to succeed alone, by cultural narratives that demonized single women as pathetic or incomplete, and by legal structures that ensured women remained financially dependent on men. It was never about love, never about companionship, never about mutual respect, it was about control. They built a system where women were forced to attach themselves to men, not because men provided anything of real value, but because the alternative was economic ruin. They created a world where a woman alone was vulnerable, not because she was incapable of survival, but because men deliberately hoarded resources and power to ensure she could not thrive without them. But the lie is unraveling. Women are proving, every day, that they do not need marriage to survive. In fact, they are often better off without it.

Financially, women who avoid marriage are saving more, investing more, and maintaining greater economic independence than their married counterparts. The data is clear: single women build more wealth, while married women often find themselves in financial situations that disproportionately benefit their husbands. How many women have sacrificed promotions, taken on part-time work, or given up their own ambitions to accommodate a husband's career? How many have found themselves managing all the unpaid labor of a household while their husbands enjoy the full benefit of two incomes? The so-called financial security of marriage has always been a security for men, not for women. Women who avoid marriage keep full control over their earnings, their property, their future. They are not forced to make economic decisions based on a partner who may leave, may fail, may burden them with debt or financial instability. They are not funneled into a legal structure designed to keep them financially tethered to men who, more often than not, contribute little to their actual well-being.

And what about support? Marriage is sold as a safety net, as if having a husband automatically ensures care and companionship. But who, exactly, is doing the caretaking in these marriages? It is women. Women are the ones caring for sick husbands, managing the household, keeping everything running smoothly while men simply expect to be served. Men are not the safety net. Women are. And when women escape marriage, they learn that they can create their own support systems, ones that do not rely on men who expect everything and give nothing. They realize that true support does not come from an institution built to trap them but from the relationships they build outside of it.

This is why more women are choosing alternative models of community and support. They are living together, sharing homes and expenses, raising children as co-parents and extended families rather than nuclear households centered around men. They are forming tight-knit networks of friends who provide emotional and practical support, a sisterhood that does not disappear just because a man decides he no longer finds his wife useful. They are building structures that prioritize them, that are not dictated by legal contracts designed to keep them bound to men, that are rooted in reciprocity rather than obligation. Because women do not need husbands. They need community, they need equity, they need the freedom to live without the constraints of marriage, without the expectation that they must sacrifice their own comfort, security, and future just to maintain the illusion of stability that marriage falsely promises.

And let's address the greatest fear the marriage-industrial complex has instilled in women: But what about old age? Who will take care of you? The answer is simple: the same people who take care of elderly married women, other women. Look at nursing homes, hospitals, and caregiving professions. It is women who do the work, whether they are married or not. Men, statistically, do not take care of their wives in old age. They do not become caregivers. In fact, elderly married women are often burdened with taking care of sick husbands while receiving little to no care themselves. A lifetime of servitude, of making meals, of washing clothes, of providing emotional and physical labor, and what do they receive in return? A husband who will never do the same. A husband who, when he falls ill, expects his wife to serve him until her last breath. Meanwhile, elderly single women who have built strong social ties, maintained financial independence, and cultivated community bonds are thriving. They are traveling, engaging in hobbies, forming interdependent networks that ensure they are never isolated. They are not trapped in a house with a man who sees them as a caretaker. They are not burdened by the demands of a marriage that has long since stopped serving them.

Marriage does not provide survival, women do. Women provide for each other. Women care for each other. Women build the networks that sustain life. Men do not create these structures. They do not maintain them. They do not invest in them. And once women see that they can do all of this without a husband dragging them down, they never look back. Because the lie of marriage, the myth of safety, the promise of support, has always been a deception designed to keep women trapped. And now, women are choosing something better. A life that is theirs, a future that belongs to them, a world where husbands are no longer needed, because they never were.

A future without husbands is not just possible, it is already happening. More women than ever are refusing to marry, delaying marriage indefinitely, or walking away from their marriages after realizing that husbands do not add value to their lives. And instead of the lonely, tragic existence that men and society warned them about, they are happier, freer, wealthier, and more fulfilled than their married counterparts. The warnings about single women dying alone, about regretting their choices, about missing out on some supposed deep fulfillment have all been exposed as lies meant to keep women tethered to men. The reality is that women who reject marriage are living lives that men envy, autonomous, unburdened, full of possibility. They are traveling, thriving in careers, deepening their friendships, building chosen families, and securing their own futures. They are proving, with every passing year, that marriage was never the key to happiness. It was the cage.

The idea that women need husbands to build a future was always a lie. The truth is, the institution of marriage was never about ensuring women's happiness or security. It was about securing male access to female labor, domestic, emotional, sexual, and reproductive. Marriage was never designed for women's benefit. It was designed to ensure that men were never alone, that they always had someone to take care of them, that they could pass their responsibilities onto a wife while still receiving the privileges of male autonomy. It was built to lock women into a life of unpaid service, to ensure that no matter how far women advanced in education, in careers, in personal independence, they would always be dragged back to the role of caretaker, bound by legal and financial ties to a man who would never be expected to reciprocate.

But women are rejecting this role, and the world is beginning to shift. Instead of dreaming of weddings, women are dreaming of financial independence, travel, career success, deep friendships, and chosen family. Instead of planning lives around men, women are planning lives around themselves. They are prioritizing their own goals, their own desires, their own futures, and they are thriving. They are choosing homes that are designed for their comfort, not for a man's convenience. They are making financial decisions that prioritize their independence, not a husband's control. They are raising children in supportive communities, rather than isolating themselves in nuclear family structures that overburden them with unpaid labor. They are creating new models of living that do not rely on marriage, on partnership, on the false promise that a man will someday take care of them. Because they have finally realized that men were never taking care of them, women were taking care of men.

And for women who do want love, companionship, or intimacy? They can still have it, on their own terms. A world without husbands does not mean a world without relationships. It means a world where relationships are chosen, not forced. Where women can engage in companionship without legal or financial entrapment. Where women can love and be loved without sacrificing their freedom. It means relationships where both people contribute equally, where women are not expected to mother their partners, where love is not tied to obligation. It means a world where women never again have to endure loveless, exhausting marriages just to survive.

Men, of course, hate this idea. They do not fear the end of marriage because they love women and want deep, meaningful partnerships. They fear it because they know that without marriage, they will have to offer something of real value to be chosen. They will have to evolve, to work, to contribute, to actually be equal partners. And many of them simply do not know how. For generations, they have been able to coast through relationships, offering nothing but the bare minimum, expecting women to do all the work of love, of care, of making a home. Now, that model is crumbling, and they are faced with a reality they never prepared for, a world where women do not need them.

But that is not women's problem to solve. Women have spent centuries contorting themselves to fit the role of wife, a role that benefits men while exhausting women. Now, they are choosing something different. They are choosing sisterhood over servitude. They are choosing independence over obligation. They are choosing a future where husbands are no longer a requirement, but an option that few will take. And men will have to face the consequences of their own neglect, their own entitlement, their own failure to be the kind of partners that women would actually want to build a life with.

And as more women wake up to this reality, the future becomes clear: we never needed husbands. They needed us. And now, they will have to face what they have always feared most, a world where women are truly free.

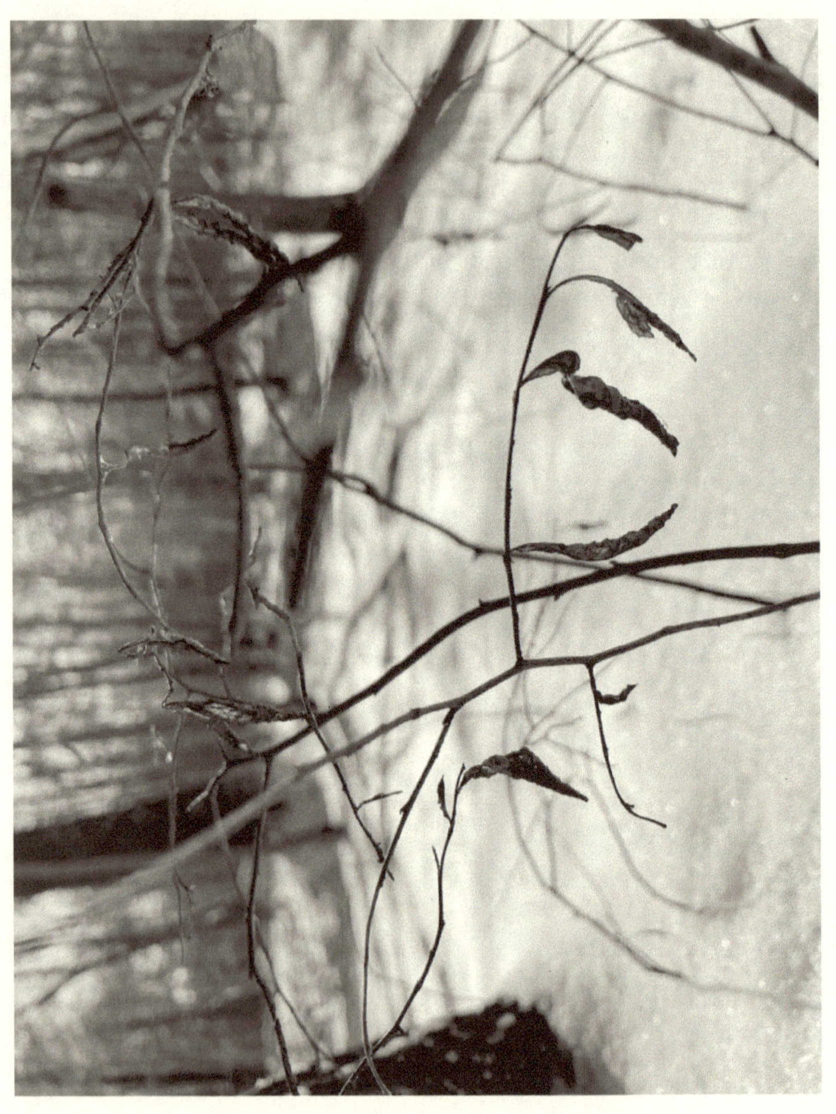

Section 4
Do Not Have Children with Men – End the Bloodline of Patriarchy

~10
The Birth Strike – Stop Producing Their Soldiers
Every Son We Bear Could Become an Oppressor

Women have been told for centuries that bearing children is their highest calling, their greatest purpose, their natural duty. But they were never told the full truth, that childbirth is not just about continuing a family line. It is about continuing their power. It is about reproducing the system that keeps men in control. It is about creating the next generation of oppressors, enforcers, and patriarchs. Every woman who gives birth is not just bringing a child into the world; she is potentially bringing in another cog for the machine, another enforcer of the very structures that have kept her subjugated. The state does not care about the beauty of motherhood, about the bond between a mother and her child, about the love that women pour into their children. The state cares about replenishing its workforce, about securing future soldiers, about ensuring that men will always have women dependent on them. This is why they panic when women refuse. Because it is not about family, it is about power.

For every daughter we birth into this world, we risk bringing another girl into suffering, another girl who will grow up in a society that sees her as less valuable, who will be told to shrink herself, to be accommodating, to prioritize everyone else's comfort above her own. She will be raised in a world that will sexualize her before she understands what that means, that will tell her she must be pleasing, that will teach her through laws, through culture, through casual dismissal, that her autonomy will always be negotiable. She will grow up knowing that her safety is conditional, that her rights can be stripped away at any moment, that her worth will always be measured against her ability to serve others. And for every son we birth? We risk raising another man who will see women as lesser. Another man who will inherit male privilege, male entitlement, and male violence simply by existing in a world that rewards him for it. A son who, no matter how much his mother tries, will absorb the silent lessons of the world, that men lead and women follow, that men deserve and women give, that power is his by birthright. No matter how much we love them, no matter how hard we try, patriarchy seeps into them.

This is the part they never tell us. They sell us the dream of motherhood as an act of love, as a sacred bond, as something that will complete us. But the reality is far darker. When a woman gives birth to a son, she cannot protect him from the lessons the world will teach him. No matter how much she tries to raise him to be different, he will see how the world treats men and women, and he will adapt. He will see men in power, men making decisions, men being respected and obeyed while women are dismissed, degraded, and discarded. And unless she fights every single day to undo this conditioning, he will absorb it. She will watch as he learns, not through her words, but through his own lived experience, that his male peers are given more respect, that they are encouraged to take up space, that the world will always cater to them in ways it never will for women. She will try to fight it. She will teach him about justice, about equality, about kindness. And yet, how many times have we seen it fail?

How many of us have seen this happen? How many women have raised sons with love, with care, with feminist values, only to watch them grow into the same men who ignore women in meetings, who laugh at misogynistic jokes, who date women half their age, who marry expecting a servant, who never once question the system that benefits them? How many mothers have poured their energy into raising "good men" only to watch those sons grow up to defend rapists, to support oppressive laws, to see women's suffering as a distant, abstract issue that does not concern them? How many mothers have tried to raise their sons differently, only to see them slowly conform to the expectations placed upon them by other men? This is the reality of reproduction under patriarchy. It does not matter how much love a woman gives her child if the world will teach him that his power is more important than her dignity.

This is why the birth strike is not just a protest, it is an act of war. The greatest weapon patriarchy has is women's willingness to keep producing its foot soldiers. Every generation of men who rule over us, who strip our rights, who laugh in our faces as they pass laws against our bodies, who rape and abuse and exploit and kill, they were all born by women. They were all raised by women who believed that this time, maybe, things would be different. That if they just loved them enough, if they just taught them the right values, if they just showed them how to respect women, they would not become part of the machine. But nothing will change if we keep playing their game. If we keep bringing more men into this world, into a system that rewards them for being our oppressors.

They do not deserve more sons. They do not deserve the future we would give them. They do not deserve another generation of men who will inherit the power their fathers stole from us. The only way to end this cycle is to stop participating in it altogether. If men will not change, if they will not dismantle the structures that have kept women subjugated, then women must make the only choice left to them, to refuse. No more soldiers for patriarchy. No more heirs to the throne. No more men born into a world that will teach them to rule over us. The next generation will not be their successors. The next generation will not be given to them.

The bloodline of oppression ends with us.

They Don't Care If We Die in Childbirth

They do not care if we die. They never have. The women who bled out on delivery tables, the women whose bodies were torn apart bringing new life into the world, the women who screamed for help while doctors ignored their pain, they were all acceptable losses in the machine of patriarchy. The only thing that ever mattered was the continuation of male bloodlines, the production of more workers, more soldiers, more men to inherit power. The suffering, the death, the irreversible damage inflicted on women's bodies, these were not tragic consequences, not failures of the system, but necessary sacrifices to keep men's world intact. A woman's body was always seen as a resource, something to be used up and discarded, something that existed not for her own sake but to ensure the survival of those who would inherit control.

And if women suffer? If women die? If women's bodies are destroyed in the process? That has never been their concern. Look at the numbers. The United States has the highest maternal mortality rate in the developed world, a crisis made even more deadly for Black women, whose pain and suffering are so dismissed by the medical system that they are three times more likely to die during childbirth. These are not isolated tragedies. These are not mere oversights in a system that is otherwise designed to protect life. These are patterns. These are policies. These are the inevitable consequences of a world that never saw women's survival as a priority. They will claim these deaths are regrettable, they will pretend to be shocked by the statistics, they will act as though they are only now realizing how dangerous pregnancy has become. But the truth is, it has always been this way. They have always known. And they have never cared.

Doctors once refused to use anesthesia on women in labor because they believed pain was part of the process, a punishment from God. Slave owners forced Black women to bear children they did not want so they could increase their profits, treating their bodies as nothing more than breeding stock. The Catholic Church still teaches that women's purpose is to produce children, even if it kills them. The suffering of women in childbirth is not an unfortunate side effect, it is a built-in feature of the system. It was never about protecting life, never about ensuring the well-being of mothers or children. It was always about control. It was always about ensuring that women remained bound to men, bound to the state, bound to a biological function that could be used against them at every turn.

Even now, as abortion rights are stripped away, as hospitals refuse life-saving care because of fear of legal consequences, women are dying preventable deaths. Women who have miscarriages are being denied medical treatment because doctors are afraid to act. Women with life-threatening pregnancies are being told to just "wait and see" while they deteriorate. Women are being forced to carry non-viable pregnancies that will kill them because the law prioritizes a fetus over the woman carrying it. And still, the men who enforce these policies, who sit in courtrooms and pass these laws, who claim to be the moral leaders of society, have the audacity to demand children from us. They expect us to risk our lives so they can have a legacy, so they can pass down their names, so they can ensure another generation of men exists to carry on their power.

But we are saying no. No more risking our lives to bring their children into this world. No more suffering so they can have a future. No more sacrificing our bodies, our health, our autonomy for a system that sees us as disposable. If they want children so badly, let them figure out another way. Let them build artificial wombs, let them carry the burden for once, let them risk their own lives. But we are done dying for them.

This is what they fear the most, not just that women will refuse to marry, refuse to have sex, refuse to participate in their system, but that women will refuse to create the next generation of men. That we will cut off their bloodline completely. That they will be forced to watch as their name, their lineage, their so-called legacy dies because the women they have oppressed for so long simply refused to give them another chance. They know that without women's participation, without women's compliance, their power vanishes. They know that they cannot legislate us into giving birth, that they cannot force us to bring another generation into the world, that if women stop, if we truly stop, there is nothing they can do to save themselves.

And they should be afraid. Because we are not willing to die for them anymore. We are not willing to carry their children, to risk our lives, to go through agonizing pain just so they can pass down their name to another generation of oppressors. We are not willing to continue sacrificing ourselves for a world that has only ever taken from us.

They built a world that does not value us. Now, they can live in it without us.

When women say no, truly, collectively, and permanently, to bearing children for men, the consequences are immediate and irreversible. Their bloodlines end. Their power structures, built on inheritance, male dominance, and the forced passage of wealth and property through sons, begin to crumble. The lineage they counted on, the patriarchal system they expected to outlive them, the very foundation of their legacy, it vanishes. Without women willing to participate, without wombs to sustain their dynasties, patriarchy has no future. They can pass laws, they can restrict abortion, they can try to shame, coerce, and threaten us, but they cannot force us to have children. And this is what terrifies them the most: the realization that for all their power, all their money, all their brute force, they are still dependent on women to sustain their existence.

And as more women refuse, the long-term consequences for men become unavoidable. They will watch as their family names disappear, as their genetic legacies rot, as their ability to claim ownership over the next generation evaporates. The men who expected to be fathers, grandfathers, patriarchs of great dynasties will instead be the last in their line, their names buried with them, forgotten, erased from history by their own failures. This is already happening. Birth rates are plummeting. More women than ever are choosing to be child-free, seeing through the lie that motherhood is an obligation rather than a choice. In countries where women's rights have been rolled back, where abortion has been criminalized and contraception restricted, birth rates are falling even faster. The punishment for treating women as disposable, for reducing them to vessels, for thinking they could legislate us into submission is simple: extinction.

And the response from men and the state is exactly what we expect: panic. Look at the policies being proposed, forced birth, financial penalties for child-free women, restrictions on birth control, even talk of criminalizing women who refuse to marry or reproduce. They are grasping at every possible way to drag women back into forced motherhood because they know that if they cannot, they will not survive. Their power, their system, their ability to control women depends on us giving them sons. They need women to keep birthing the labor force, the foot soldiers, the next generation of enforcers. They need women to create more men who will inherit the entitlement of their fathers, more daughters who will be raised to serve. And when we stop? When we refuse? When we let their legacies end with them?

We win.

Because this is not just about numbers, it is about power. Every child we refuse to bear is one less worker for their capitalist machine. One less soldier for their imperialist wars. One less man to enforce their laws, their religions, their control. Every time a woman says no to reproduction, she is breaking a link in the chain that has kept women enslaved for generations. She is refusing to bring another oppressor into the world, refusing to create another enforcer of patriarchy. And as more women say no, the chain itself begins to disintegrate. The entire structure of control weakens. The entire machinery of patriarchy grinds to a halt.

Men will have to face the future they created. A future where they are alone. Where they have no heirs, no descendants, no one to carry on their name. Where they are left to watch as the world moves on without them, as women build something new, something better, something free from their control. A world where their bloodlines vanish, their influence fades, their carefully designed systems of power collapse under the weight of their own irrelevance. They will look around and see only the consequences of their own greed, their own selfishness, their own insistence that women exist only to serve them.

And they will try to stop us. They will scream about declining birth rates, about the collapse of civilization, about the need to "restore family values." But this is not about civilization, it is about them losing control. They fear a world where women have complete autonomy, where we are no longer bound to them by marriage, by children, by obligation. They fear a world where we have no reason to tolerate them at all. Because once women fully realize that we do not need them, not as husbands, not as fathers, not as protectors, not as rulers, they know they will be left behind.

And that world is already forming. More women are choosing themselves over motherhood, choosing freedom over duty, choosing to live on their own terms rather than be used as breeding stock for a system that does not care if they live or die. More women are refusing to waste their lives on men who contribute nothing, refusing to carry generations of ungrateful sons on their backs, refusing to sacrifice their health, their futures, their dreams for a system that only drains them.

So let their bloodlines collapse. Let their names disappear. Let them lie awake at night, knowing that they are the last of their kind, that their empire is crumbling, that they will leave no mark on the future. Let them watch as the world continues without them, as women create a future that is not theirs to control. Because that is what they deserve. A world without heirs. A world without control. A world where women finally, completely, and permanently say no.

~11

The Economy is Built on Women's Wombs

Capitalism Needs Women to Birth and Raise the Workforce

Every economic system that has ever existed has depended on one thing: women's unpaid labor. And at the center of that unpaid labor is reproduction, the expectation that women will give birth, raise children, and provide the next generation of workers, soldiers, and consumers without asking for anything in return. Capitalism was built on the assumption that women would continue to do this work indefinitely, that they would birth the labor force, sustain it, and replace it without ever demanding compensation, recognition, or even the basic conditions for survival. The entire structure of the economy would collapse if women stopped having children. And that is exactly why they are so desperate to force us to continue.

Men love to talk about the economy as if it is some abstract force, something natural, something inevitable. But capitalism is not a neutral system, it is a machine fueled by women's bodies. Every child born is a future worker who will generate profits for the ruling class. Every mother struggling to raise children on her own is another woman forced into low-wage labor, debt, and economic dependence. Every woman who is denied birth control, denied abortion, denied the choice to say no is another cog in the machine, another forced participant in the endless cycle of labor and exploitation. This is why the state does not invest in childcare, in maternal healthcare, in paid family leave. Because the entire economy depends on women doing this work for free. They do not care about children. They do not care about families. If they did, they would have built a system that supports them. Instead, they have built a system that ensures that the moment a child is born, the mother is left to fend for herself.

The second a child is born, the state's concern disappears. Suddenly, there is no universal childcare, no paid maternity leave, no healthcare guarantees, no affordable housing or education. The message is clear: our job was to produce the child, what happens after that is our problem. The economy needs a labor force, and it has always relied on women to provide one, even as it refuses to ensure that the conditions of that labor force are humane. It is why education is gutted, why wages are stagnant, why the cost of living rises while social services are slashed. It is a machine designed to exploit, to take without giving, to ensure that those in power continue to reap the benefits while those who birth, raise, and sustain the population are left in precarity.

And what happens to women who refuse to participate? They are shamed, punished, economically penalized, and socially ostracized. Women who choose not to have children are called selfish, unnatural, failures to their families and communities. Governments introduce tax breaks and financial incentives to bribe women into reproducing. Right-wing politicians push policies designed to restrict abortion and contraception, forcing women into motherhood whether they want it or not. In countries facing population decline, we are already seeing pro-natalist policies designed to pressure women back into the role of breeder, as if our purpose in life is to sustain their economy. They will legislate, manipulate, and guilt us into compliance, not because they care about children, but because they care about control.

And yet, men, the same men who depend on women to birth the workforce, contribute nothing to this labor. They do not carry the physical burden of pregnancy. They do not face the health risks, the career setbacks, the financial instability. They do not raise the children they demand be born. They do not do the parenting, the schooling, the emotional labor, the unpaid work that keeps capitalism running. They simply sit back and reap the benefits. They build wealth off the backs of mothers, while refusing to be present parents. They shape laws that strip women of reproductive rights, while taking no responsibility for the children they create. And when women struggle, when they burn out, when they break under the weight of it all, they are blamed for failing to hold up a system that was always rigged against them.

But the moment women say no? The moment we refuse to birth their next generation of workers? The panic begins. Politicians cry about declining birth rates. Corporations worry about future labor shortages. Conservative leaders push for policies that would trap women back into forced motherhood. They panic because they know that without our wombs, the entire system collapses.

And that is exactly why we must refuse. Because capitalism has taken everything from us, our labor, our time, our freedom, our health. It has used us, drained us, discarded us, and expected us to continue participating. But now, we know better. Now, we see the truth. And we owe it nothing.

Why We Owe Them Nothing

Women have been forced to give everything, our labor, our bodies, our time, our energy, our very lives, to sustain a system that does nothing for us in return. Capitalism does not reward mothers. It exploits them. It demands their unpaid labor while giving them nothing but exhaustion, financial insecurity, and social blame if they dare to struggle under the weight of it all. Women are expected to give birth, to raise children, to nurture the next generation of workers and soldiers, while receiving no structural support, no relief, no acknowledgment of the price they pay. They are told that motherhood is the most important job in the world, yet the very society that says this will discard them the moment they can no longer provide. And now, as more women begin to see the truth, as more women refuse to participate, the panic is setting in.

Governments are terrified of declining birth rates, not because they care about families, but because they need a constant supply of workers, taxpayers, and soldiers. The economy must be fed, the military must be staffed, and the consumer class must keep growing. The state does not see babies as human lives; it sees them as future economic units, future tools of production, future cannon fodder for wars they will have no choice but to fight. And for centuries, they have relied on women's compliance to keep this machine running. They counted on women being too exhausted, too indoctrinated, too trapped to ever question their role. They assumed we would keep birthing their workforce without protest. But now, for the first time in history, women are looking at this deal and saying no. No to being used, no to being drained, no to spending a lifetime in servitude to a system that has never served them.

Because we owe them nothing.

We do not owe them our wombs. We do not owe them our futures. We do not owe them sons to carry on their names or daughters to serve as the next generation of caretakers. We do not owe them our suffering so they can continue to profit. And what have they ever given in return? No paid maternity leave. No universal childcare. No free healthcare. No support at all. Women who become mothers are penalized in the workplace, earning less money while doing more work, shouldering an impossible burden while men congratulate themselves for doing the bare minimum.

A man changes one diaper, and he is called a good father. A woman spends twenty years of her life raising a child with no support, and she is told she should have made better choices. Mothers are expected to handle childcare, housework, and full-time employment, all while men contribute nothing and expect praise for merely existing in the home. And if a woman dares to struggle under the crushing weight of these expectations? She is blamed. She is told she should have planned better, should have worked harder, should have been smarter.

This is how capitalism gaslights women into servitude. It convinces them that if they are struggling, it is their own fault, not the fault of a system that was never designed to support them. It makes them feel guilty for not being able to "do it all," when in reality, "doing it all" was always an impossible, unfair expectation. It tells women they must sacrifice everything for their children, then leaves them to suffer alone when they do. It tells women that if they cannot afford to raise a child, they are failures, but if they try to avoid pregnancy, they are selfish. It ensures that no matter what women do, they are always wrong, always lacking, always at fault for the pain that has been inflicted upon them. And this is why women are walking away.

Women are choosing themselves over a system that has never chosen them. They are refusing to become mothers, refusing to birth children who will only be used as fuel for a machine that does not care if they live or die. They are rejecting the idea that they must sacrifice their bodies, their ambitions, their freedom for a society that offers them nothing in return. They are refusing to repeat the mistakes of the women who came before them, the ones who were trapped, who were abandoned, who were left exhausted and broken with nothing to show for it. And in doing so, they are unraveling the very fabric of a world that has taken them for granted.

And men? They panic. They insult child-free women, call them selfish, tell them they will die alone. They rage about declining birth rates, about the death of the traditional family, about women who refuse to do their part. They are terrified, because for the first time, they are realizing that they were never the ones in control. They only had power because women kept giving it to them. And now, women are taking it back. They are choosing their own futures, their own desires, their own ambitions. They are refusing to be tools, to be resources, to be used and discarded. They are realizing their true power, the power to refuse. The power to say, "This system does not serve me, so I will not serve it."

This is not selfishness. This is survival. And for the first time, women are choosing themselves over the demands of a system that has bled them dry for centuries.

The Future of Reproduction – If We Choose It

The greatest fear of patriarchy, capitalism, and the state is that women will realize that we do not have to reproduce. That we do not have to create the next generation of workers, soldiers, and servants. That our wombs are not public property, that our bodies are not factories to fuel the machine. For centuries, they have relied on the assumption that women would continue to have babies, no matter how little we were given in return. They built economies, societies, entire nations on the unpaid labor of mothers, on the silent suffering of women who were forced to birth and raise children with no support, no security, no control over their own lives. They assumed that women's biological capacity to bear children meant an obligation to do so. They assumed we would never refuse. But now, as more women reject forced motherhood, as birth rates plummet in countries that treat women as second-class citizens, we are seeing the cracks form. The system is failing, and their desperation is growing.

And that is why the conversation is shifting from whether we should reproduce to if and how we choose to do so. Because reproduction should never have been about duty or obligation. It should have been about choice. And for the first time, women are demanding that choice be on our terms, not men's, not the state's, not capitalism's. They are realizing that their value is not tied to their ability to create life, that their futures do not have to be defined by motherhood, that they do not have to give birth just because it is expected of them. And what does a future of reproduction by choice, not by force, look like?

It looks like women deciding who, when, and if they will reproduce, not based on guilt, shame, or pressure, but based on what is best for them. It looks like women refusing to bring children into a world that does not support them, refusing to birth children into poverty, environmental collapse, and state violence. It looks like women demanding that if society wants a new generation, it must prove that it is worth bringing children into. No more forced sacrifice, no more women suffering in silence while governments, corporations, and men take and take and take. If they want a future, they will have to earn it.

It means that if we choose to have children, we do so with our eyes open, with full control over the circumstances, with guarantees that we and our children will be supported. No more unpaid labor, no more thankless sacrifices, no more struggling alone while men sit back and reap the benefits. If men want children, let them prove they deserve to be fathers. Let them prove they will be equal partners, that they will carry the burden, that they will not treat women as disposable incubators. Let them prove that they will raise sons who are not oppressors, who do not grow up entitled to women's labor and bodies. Let them prove that they are worthy of parenthood, that they will not disappear the moment the child is born, that they will not leave women to suffer alone while they continue to live as though nothing has changed. Until then, they get nothing.

This is the world they fear, a world where women reclaim complete control of reproduction, where their participation is neither expected nor coerced, where they do not exist as vessels to perpetuate a system that has brutalized them for centuries. It is a world where women refuse to birth the next generation of oppressors, where they do not bring sons into existence only to see them inherit the entitlement and violence of their fathers, where they do not create daughters only to watch them struggle against the same chains that bound them. It is a world where reproduction is not a duty but a choice, not a sacrifice but an act of power. And that is why the system fights so desperately to keep control, why it scrambles to restrict abortion, to attack contraception, to shut down clinics, to force women back into the role of mother whether they want it or not. They know that if women refuse to create the next generation of workers, soldiers, and caretakers, the entire foundation of their power structure crumbles.

Because without women's compliance, without the unpaid and unrecognized labor that fuels the economy, without the steady flow of new births to sustain capitalism and nationalism, they have nothing. They have always relied on women's forced participation, on the assumption that no matter how badly they treat us, no matter how much they take from us, we will still continue to reproduce. That we will still bring life into a world that has never valued ours. That we will still see pregnancy as an obligation rather than a choice. And so, their panic is not just about declining birth rates, it is about losing control. It is about realizing that for the first time, women are recognizing their own worth, their own power, their own ability to say no.

And so, the crackdown intensifies. Laws are passed to make leaving harder, to make escaping impossible, to turn back the clock to a time when women had no options outside of marriage and motherhood. They strip away reproductive rights, they criminalize abortion, they restrict contraception, they make medical care inaccessible, they stack courts with men who believe women's bodies exist for the purpose of reproduction. They will do everything in their power to drag us back, to reinstate the chains we have begun to break. Because without those chains, they know they have nothing.

But what they do not understand, what they refuse to accept, is that it is already too late. The birth strike is real, the refusal is growing, and every day, more women are waking up to the reality that they do not owe men their bodies, do not owe the state their fertility, do not owe society their compliance. Women are choosing themselves, choosing lives where they are not exhausted, depleted, and broken by the demands of men who see them as nothing more than vessels for the next generation. They are recognizing that to refuse motherhood under patriarchy is not selfish, it is an act of defiance, of resistance, of self-preservation.

And the more men refuse to change, the more they cling to their desperate belief that women can still be controlled, the more they will be forced to watch as their bloodlines vanish, as their power disintegrates, as the one thing they thought they could always depend on, women's willingness to serve, disappears entirely. Because the future is no longer theirs to dictate. If women choose to have children, it will not be to fuel their system, to sustain their empires, to keep their institutions alive. It will be for women, by women, in a world where women, not men, define what comes next.

And if men cannot handle that? If they rage, if they panic, if they legislate, if they beg? Let them. It will change nothing. The choice has already been made. And we are never going back.

~12

Building a World Without Male Dependence

How Women Can Thrive Without Bearing Children

For centuries, women have been told that their value is tied to their ability to reproduce. That their purpose is to bear children, to raise them, to sacrifice themselves for the next generation. That without motherhood, they are incomplete, unfulfilled, or worse, selfish. Every institution, from the family to the state, from religion to economics, has reinforced this idea, ensuring that women feel obligated to continue the cycle. But now, women are rejecting this lie. They are seeing that a life without children is not a life of loss, but a life of freedom, fulfillment, and limitless possibility. They are realizing that their existence is not defined by what they can give to others but by what they can create for themselves. And in doing so, they are breaking the foundation upon which patriarchy has stood for centuries.

The greatest fear of patriarchy is that women will thrive without it. That women will see husbands not as providers, but as burdens. That they will understand that they do not need children to have purpose. That they will walk away from the role assigned to them and never return. The world has always functioned under the assumption that women will dedicate their lives to serving men, to raising future workers, to producing the next generation of enforcers for the very system that exploits them. But what happens when women refuse? What happens when they choose themselves over duty, over obligation, over the expectation that they must be mothers before they can be anything else? What happens when they see motherhood not as inevitable, but as a choice they are free to reject?

The answer is already unfolding. More and more women are choosing child-free lives, and the benefits are undeniable. Without the physical, financial, and emotional burden of motherhood, women are able to pursue careers, travel, form deeper friendships, engage in activism, build wealth, and prioritize their own well-being. They are no longer trapped in nuclear families that isolate them, no longer forced into caregiving roles that deplete them, no longer tied to men who refuse to share the burdens of parenting. They are discovering that their lives have meaning beyond what they can provide for others. They are choosing paths that were once denied to them, paths that allow them to be whole, independent, untethered from a system that has only taken from them.

And the backlash is immediate. Men rage about declining birth rates, about "selfish women," about the death of the traditional family. Politicians panic, governments scramble to find ways to force women back into reproduction, to incentivize childbirth, to legislate control over women's bodies. The church condemns them, the media shames them, their families beg them to reconsider. But their anger, their desperation, their fury is not about women's choices, it is about losing control. They are afraid because they know that a world where women no longer bear their children is a world where women no longer depend on them. And when women no longer depend on men, men lose power.

Women who refuse to have children are refusing to participate in a system that takes everything from them and gives nothing back. They are refusing to sacrifice their bodies, their futures, their freedom for men who see them as nothing more than incubators. They are refusing to give birth to sons who will be taught to oppress them. They are refusing to create the next generation of men who will inherit their fathers' entitlement, their fathers' violence, their fathers' belief that women exist to serve them. They are walking away, and the system is crumbling without them.

And for the first time, women are creating alternative models of survival. They are forming chosen families, living with friends, pooling resources, sharing responsibilities. They are building wealth instead of passing it down to ungrateful sons. They are investing in their futures, making plans for old age that do not depend on children to take care of them. They are proving that women who choose themselves do not end up alone, miserable, or lost. They end up thriving. They end up in community, in joy, in lives that belong only to them.

This is the world men never wanted to see. A world where women are happy without them. A world where women have no reason to look back, to regret, to long for what was never meant to serve them in the first place. A world where men become irrelevant, unnecessary, forgotten. And every day, more women are stepping into this world, realizing that their life was never meant to be spent in service to men or to the next generation of men. Every day, another woman chooses herself.

We are the generation breaking the cycle. We are the generation refusing to live for others. We are the generation showing future women that there is a path beyond motherhood, beyond sacrifice, beyond servitude. And that path leads to something patriarchy never prepared for: women living for themselves, and never looking back.

Breaking the Cycle of Abuse and Trauma

Women have been trapped in a cycle of abuse, trauma, and forced obligation for generations. Every system, patriarchy, religion, capitalism, the nuclear family, has been carefully designed to keep them in a state of dependence, subservience, and exhaustion. These systems do not simply exist; they have been deliberately crafted, reinforced over centuries, and woven so deeply into society that women have been conditioned to believe that suffering is their natural state. The expectation has always been clear: women will endure. Women will suffer in silence. Women will push through the pain, the neglect, the mistreatment, because that is what women have always done.

They have been told to sacrifice themselves for the greater good, for their families, for their husbands, for their children, for a society that gives them nothing in return. Every culture, every institution, every moral doctrine has insisted that a woman's value is measured by how much she is willing to bear. The idea that she might refuse has been so unimaginable, so threatening, that entire religions have been built around punishing women who attempt to escape. But now, women are refusing. And in that refusal, everything begins to unravel.

What happens when women walk away from toxic families, from abusive relationships, from societal expectations that demand they keep sacrificing? What happens when they decide that they do not owe men their time, their energy, their emotional labor, or their wombs? The system panics. The men who have relied on their unpaid labor panic. The families who have drained them without reciprocity panic. The very structure of power shakes.

Because the entire system is built on women's willingness to stay. It is built on the assumption that no matter how much they are harmed, they will continue to return, continue to forgive, continue to try. Women have been told that they must keep their families intact, that they must prioritize the feelings of men over their own survival, that they must raise children even when doing so will destroy them. But now, for the first time, more and more women are breaking free. And the system does not know how to function without them.

One of the most effective ways men have maintained control over women is through intergenerational trauma. They have used motherhood as a tool, not simply to continue their lineage but to ensure the survival of their power. They have relied on women to birth sons who will become oppressors and daughters who will accept oppression. They have treated childbirth not as an act of creation but as a mechanism of control, a way to ensure that the next generation is indoctrinated before they even have a chance to resist. And for those who dare to reject this cycle, who refuse to birth the next generation of enforcers, the punishment is swift. They are shamed, ostracized, labeled as unnatural, as selfish, as broken. Because nothing terrifies men more than the idea that women will stop producing their successors. Nothing frightens them more than the thought that the power they have taken for granted might end with them.

Women have been told for centuries that family is everything, that they should forgive the men who abused them, that they should stay in marriages for the sake of their children, that they should tolerate mistreatment because "that's just how men are." They have been told that love is endurance, that loyalty is suffering, that their purpose is to nurture, no matter how much it costs them. They have been conditioned to believe that to walk away is to fail, that to demand more is selfish, that to prioritize their own lives is unnatural.

But we are the generation breaking that cycle. More and more women are choosing to walk away from abusive families, to cut ties with men who drain them, to refuse to carry the trauma of previous generations. They are refusing to be the emotional shock absorbers for broken men who refuse to heal themselves. They are refusing to stay in relationships where they are treated as servants rather than equals.

And this shift is terrifying to men because they have always counted on women's tolerance. They have always assumed that women would stay no matter how bad it gets, that they would continue to pour themselves into relationships that only take from them, that they would keep forgiving, keep mothering, keep absorbing all the damage that men refuse to acknowledge. But now, women are realizing that they do not have to. And in that realization, men are seeing their own power slip away.

Women are healing on their own terms. They are finding community in sisterhood, in chosen families, in friendships that do not demand endless sacrifice. They are seeking therapy, building financial independence, refusing to accept men as unfinished projects who need to be fixed. They are prioritizing their own well-being instead of constantly managing men's emotions. They are rejecting the idea that love is suffering, that relationships are endurance tests, that their purpose is to soothe men's egos and clean up their messes. And in doing so, they are closing the door on generations of abuse. They are saying, no more. Not me. Not my life. Not my future.

This is what real freedom looks like, walking away from men and systems that only seek to use and discard us. This is how we break the cycle, by refusing to birth another generation of women who will be told to suffer quietly, by refusing to raise another generation of men who believe that suffering is a woman's duty. This is how we dismantle patriarchy, not through protest alone, not through endless attempts at reforming a system that was never meant to be fair to us, but through absolute, unwavering refusal.

And the more women who refuse, the more the foundation of patriarchy crumbles. Because men have built their entire world on the assumption that women will always come back. That we will always endure. That we will never leave. But we are leaving. And we are never coming back.

What a True Pro-Woman Future Would Look Like

A world that truly prioritizes women does not resemble the one we live in now. It is not a world where women are expected to serve, sacrifice, and endure while men take, exploit, and rule. It is not a world where women are defined by their relationships to men, where their worth is measured by their ability to be wives, mothers, or caregivers. A world that prioritizes women is one where they are fully autonomous, fully in control, and fully free. It is a world where their existence is not framed through the lens of what they can provide for men, but by the lives they build for themselves, for each other, for a future that is not dictated by male entitlement.

For centuries, men have shaped the world in their image, designing laws, economies, and social structures that serve their needs while demanding that women work tirelessly to uphold them. They have written history as if they alone built civilization, as if every system of power, every technological advancement, every political order was the result of their genius rather than the unpaid labor of women, the silent sacrifice of those who were never allowed to claim ownership over the worlds they created. But women are no longer interested in merely surviving within a system that was never built for them. We are here to create something new. We are here to dismantle every institution that has served only to keep us tethered to men's ambitions, to rip apart every narrative that has told us we must live for others, that our value is dependent on what we provide rather than who we are.

A truly pro-woman future is one where women never have to depend on men for survival. It is a future where women control their own finances, their own homes, their own futures. Where marriage is obsolete, no longer an expectation forced upon women as a means of legal and financial security. Where reproduction is a choice, not an obligation, and no woman is coerced into motherhood for the sake of the economy, the state, or the insecurities of men who see their legacy as more important than women's lives. It is a world where women thrive together, supporting one another emotionally, financially, socially, where no woman is left to struggle alone, where no woman is abandoned to the isolation of a patriarchal structure that only values her if she serves a man.

This is what terrifies them the most, a world where women do not need them. For too long, men have relied on women's fear. The fear of being alone, of financial instability, of being cast out as unnatural or selfish for choosing themselves over servitude. But that fear is fading. Women are seeing that a life without male dependence is not a life of isolation, it is a life of freedom. It is a life where success is defined on women's terms, where happiness is built outside of the narrow constraints of marriage and motherhood. It is a world where women's labor is not exploited for free, where their care is not expected without reciprocity, where their suffering is no longer a prerequisite for male comfort.

A future built by and for women means breaking free from patriarchal narratives that have told us we must live for others. It means rejecting the expectation that we are here to be caretakers, to be the emotional crutches for broken men, to be the wombs that produce the next generation of men who will inherit their fathers' entitlement. It means creating a world where workplaces are structured around fairness, not male competition and exploitation.

Where healthcare systems prioritize women's well-being, providing full access to reproductive care, maternal health, and bodily autonomy without state interference, without theocratic rule dictating what women can and cannot do with their bodies. It means forming chosen families, women living together, supporting one another, ensuring that no woman is ever left without resources, without community, without power. It means an education system designed to empower women, not to prepare them to serve men.

This is not a fantasy. It is already happening. Women are choosing themselves, choosing their own futures, choosing community, choosing independence. Women are refusing to participate in a system that never cared for them. They are refusing to raise another generation of men who will inherit their father's violence, their father's entitlement, their father's disregard for women's humanity. They are refusing to settle, to stay quiet, to keep the machine running. And the more women refuse, the more the world will shift.

Men built this system under the assumption that women would never have the power to walk away. That women would always accept their place, always continue to serve, always seek validation from the very men who built a world that despised them. But they were wrong. We are walking away. And what comes next will not be built in their image. It will be built in ours.

Section 5
The Controlled Male Experiment – One Man Per Circle, The Rest Get Nothing

~13
The Chosen One
Selecting a Man to Serve Women, Not the Other Way Around

For all of history, men have operated under the assumption that women exist to serve them. In every structure of power, in every economy, in every culture, they have positioned themselves as the arbiters of worth, deciding which women deserve attention, protection, resources, and love. They have built entire civilizations on the foundation of their own entitlement, ensuring that men, regardless of their merit or contribution, would always be granted access to women's labor, companionship, and care. They have weaponized marriage, religion, and economics to enforce this system, conditioning women to believe that their survival depends on securing a man's approval. And because they have never been forced to compete in any meaningful way, because they have always been told that women would choose them no matter how little they offered, they have never had to reflect on their own shortcomings, their own mediocrity, their own failure to be worthy of the devotion they demand. But what happens when women flip the script?

If men have spent centuries selecting which women deserve marriage, sex, and security, then women can do the same. And instead of every man having automatic access to women's time, energy, and care, only the most worthy will be chosen. Enter the Controlled Male Experiment, one man per circle. Each group of women, whether a household, a community, or a network of friends, will select one man to serve them, to provide for them, to offer companionship on their terms. The rest? They get nothing. They will not be argued with, reasoned with, convinced of their inadequacy, they will simply be left out. They will be forced to watch, to reflect, to finally experience what it means to be on the outside looking in.

This is not about punishment. It is about balance. It is about rebalancing a power dynamic that has existed for far too long in one direction, about making men experience the exclusion, rejection, and dismissal that they have inflicted upon women for generations. For centuries, society has ensured that even the laziest, most incompetent, most useless men still had access to women's affection and labor. No matter how they behaved, no matter how much damage they caused, no matter how little they contributed, they were never truly alone. They never had to look at themselves and wonder why no woman would have them. They never had to feel what it means to be unwanted. But what happens when women stop playing along?

What happens when only one man per community is chosen to have access to women, chosen not because he is entitled to it, but because he has proven himself to be useful, supportive, emotionally intelligent, and dedicated to women's well-being? What happens when the vast majority of men, for the first time in their lives, understand what it means to be excluded, to be deemed unnecessary, to be shut out? The answer is simple: men will either evolve, or they will disappear.

For too long, men have assumed that women will always be there, waiting for them to grow, forgiving their failings, tolerating their incompetence. But in the Controlled Male Experiment, there are no second chances, no guarantees, no automatic privileges. The men who fail to meet the standard will not be negotiated with, will not be taught how to be better, will not be given endless opportunities to improve. They will simply be left behind. And the one man who is chosen? He will understand that he is not the center of this new dynamic. He is not the leader, the owner, the one dictating terms. He is there to serve the women who selected him, to contribute to their lives, to provide, not to extract. He will understand that his inclusion is conditional, that his access is a privilege, that he is one among many who did not make the cut.

This is what scares men the most, not just losing access to women, but losing the assumption that they will always be chosen no matter what. They have built their entire identity on the belief that they will never be alone, that no matter how they behave, some woman will still take them in, care for them, tolerate them. But now, they will finally have to earn it. And if they cannot? Then they get nothing. Just as women have gotten nothing from them for centuries.

Why This Incentive Model Will Change Men's Behavior

Men have never been forced to evolve. They have existed in a world that has demanded nothing of them beyond their mere presence, a world where their flaws are overlooked, their failures excused, their worst behaviors tolerated. They have taken for granted that no matter how selfish, how lazy, how emotionally stunted they are, there will always be a woman willing to endure them. They have built their lives on the assumption that women will always be available, that we will always compromise, that settling is simply a part of life for us. They have never had to earn the relationships they demand, the love they expect, or the support they take without gratitude. But now, the Controlled Male Experiment removes that automatic access. It shifts the power dynamic in a way they never anticipated. It forces men into a position they have never been in before: irrelevance.

Instead of every man assuming he is entitled to a woman's time, affection, and labor, only one man per group will be chosen to engage with women in any meaningful way. The rest will be left watching from the outside. And for the first time, they will have to face the brutal truth: women were the prize all along. They were never the ones with power, they were never the ones who got to decide. It was only an illusion, a structure they built to convince themselves that women needed them more than they needed women. That illusion collapses the moment women step back and say, only one of you gets in.

This incentive model will force a complete restructuring of male behavior, because for the first time, men will have to compete for something they assumed was their birthright. The average man puts in no effort to be a decent partner, friend, or ally to women because he has never had to. Women have been conditioned to accept men as they are, to make excuses for them, to absorb their flaws, to put up with their failures, to bear the burden of fixing them. But when access to women is no longer guaranteed, when women are only engaging with one carefully selected man per group, every other man will be left behind. And suddenly, the rules change.

No longer will men be able to coast through life assuming that a woman will tolerate them simply because she has no other choice. No longer will lazy, entitled, emotionally stunted men be able to rely on sheer probability to find a woman willing to settle. No longer will men who bring nothing to the table still expect a woman to serve them. Because now, the bar is not "just be slightly better than the worst men out there." The bar is now, "be among the top 1% of men or be left with nothing." That alone will send a shockwave through male behavior.

For the first time, men will have to listen. They will have to learn. They will have to put in work. Because only one of them gets access to women, and every other man will have to sit back and wonder why he was not chosen. This is not just about withholding sex or relationships. It is about forcing men to experience the consequences of their own mediocrity. Right now, men who refuse to evolve still find women willing to accept them, to carry them, to lower their standards just to avoid loneliness. But when the entire structure shifts, when women remove themselves from the equation and only allow one, carefully vetted man per group into their circle, every other man will have to face what women have always known:

that being excluded hurts, that watching others be chosen while you remain unwanted is a bitter pill to swallow, that sitting alone, without companionship, without support, without the emotional and physical benefits of women's presence, is unbearable.

And if they want access to women? If they want to be one of the rare few selected? They will have to prove it. Not with words, not with promises, not with performative "good guy" posturing, but with real, measurable change. They will have to unlearn centuries of entitlement, abandon the idea that women exist to serve them, prove that they are capable of equality, of partnership, of effort. And the ones who refuse? The ones who rage, who complain, who call it unfair, who throw tantrums because suddenly, for the first time, they are being held to a standard? They will be left exactly where they belong, alone, watching, realizing too late that they lost the only thing that ever truly mattered.

Men Have Used Women This Way for Centuries—Fair is Fair

For centuries, men have hoarded access to women, dictated the terms of our existence, and rationed out dignity as though it were theirs to give. They have decided who is worthy of marriage, who is desirable enough to be loved, who is allowed safety, stability, and security. They have constructed entire societies in which a small number of powerful men claim the best resources, the most beautiful women, the highest status, while the rest of men are left to fight among themselves for whatever remains. They have turned women into a commodity to be won, a prize to be owned, an asset to be controlled.

They have ensured that women must compete for their approval, conditioned us to believe that our worth is tied to whether or not a man chooses us. But what has been asked of men in return? Nothing. They have been granted access to women without effort, without merit, without proving themselves worthy of anything. They have built economies, religions, and cultural narratives where the only requirement for obtaining a woman's time, body, and loyalty is simply being a man. But now, the game has changed.

For the first time in history, women are controlling access to men instead of the other way around. One man per circle, the rest get nothing. This is not an act of cruelty, it is simply balance. It is an inversion of a system that has operated to our detriment for centuries. If men had no issue excluding women, deciding which women would receive privilege and which would be discarded, then they should have no issue with the same logic being applied to them. And yet, they will panic. They will rage. They will call it unfair. Because men have always assumed they will be chosen, no matter how little they contribute. They believe there is always a woman somewhere willing to tolerate them, to settle, to fix them. But what happens when there is not?

What happens when only one man per community is chosen and the rest are left to fend for themselves? What happens when women no longer look at men as a necessity but as a burden that must be justified? Men will suddenly have to compete in a way they never have before. No longer will mediocrity be rewarded with love. No longer will the mere act of existing be enough to guarantee a relationship. If they want to be chosen, they will have to rise to the occasion. They will have to bring something to the table beyond entitlement. They will have to meet the standards that women have been held to for centuries, forced to prove their worth not through words but through actions. And many of them will fail.

Men will experience the loneliness they have forced women into. They will watch as other men receive the love, care, and stability they assumed would always be theirs by default. They will understand what it feels like to be discarded, to be seen as irrelevant, to be left without access to intimacy, affection, or support. They will finally face consequences. Instead of assuming they can simply exist and still be picked, they will have to fight for something they once took for granted. And for the first time, they will know the pain of being unwanted. They will experience the desperation of trying to be seen, trying to be chosen, trying to be worthy. They will understand what it means to fight for access to something they always assumed would be given to them freely.

But this is not about revenge. It is about balance. Men created a system where women were expected to compete for resources, for love, for safety. They designed a world in which a woman's value was measured by how well she could attract and keep a man. Now, they will compete for us. And most of them will lose. Most of them will never be chosen. Most of them will be cut off from women entirely, left to wonder why they were not good enough. And that, more than anything, will force them to evolve, or disappear.

Because the reality is simple: women have always been the prize. Women have always been the ones men fought for, shaped civilizations for, wrote poetry for, waged wars over. And yet, they have never had to earn us. They have never been required to prove that they deserve our time, our energy, our devotion. But now, they do. And they are not ready for what happens next.

~14

The Last Warning – This is the Final Option

Women Have Tried Everything Else – This is the Last Option

Women have protested. Women have marched. Women have organized, voted, lobbied, and fought for every inch of progress. We have spent generations demanding justice, pleading for safety, begging for equality in a world that has refused to see us as fully human. And in return, we have been ignored, mocked, dismissed, and punished. They have treated our suffering as an inconvenience, our demands as irrational, our rights as something to be debated rather than something that belongs to us by birth. We have been told that progress takes time, that if we simply vote harder, march louder, educate more men, things will improve. We have waited through lifetimes of patience, generations of compromise, decades of sacrifice.

And yet, things have only gotten worse. Our rights have been stripped away, our bodily autonomy revoked, our futures stolen in plain sight while they tell us we are imagining it. Rapists, abusers, and predators sit at the highest levels of power, shaping the laws that govern our bodies, our lives, our choices. The economy is rigged to force us into dependence on men, yet men offer us nothing in return. We are expected to birth children who will inherit a broken world, without support, without security, without choice. We are told to be grateful for whatever crumbs they throw our way, while they gaslight us into believing that things are not as bad as they seem, even as they openly dismantle the rights we fought for, even as they strip us of our freedoms, even as they turn back the clock to a time when women had no voice at all.

This is not a world where women can negotiate their way to freedom. This is not a world where men will suddenly wake up and decide to do what is right. Men have made their intentions clear. They do not care if we suffer. They do not care if we die.

They have proven, over and over again, that our pain means nothing to them. That they would rather force us into submission than acknowledge our humanity. That they will pass laws, rig systems, and protect each other at all costs, even at the cost of our lives. They have never been interested in justice, in fairness, in equality. Their only interest has been in maintaining power, in keeping us dependent, in ensuring that we remain trapped in a system that benefits them at our expense. And they will not stop. They will not suddenly change. They will not willingly give up the control they have spent centuries consolidating.

So this is it. The last warning. The final option. We will not beg anymore. We will not negotiate. We will not wait. If men will not change, if they will not dismantle the system that benefits them while it destroys us, then we will remove ourselves from it entirely. No more participation. No more compromise. No more playing a game that was rigged from the start. Women will step back, walk away, cut them off, not just in politics, not just in workplaces, but everywhere. No more dates. No more sex. No more marriage. No more babies. Until we win. Until they have no choice but to listen.

Because this is what they fear most, not just resistance, not just opposition, but complete and total rejection. They have built a world that depends on women's participation, on our compliance, on our willingness to endure. They assume we will always be there, always trying, always forgiving, always giving, no matter how badly they treat us. But they are wrong. They have taken for granted that we will never leave. That we will never realize the full extent of our power. That we will never stop believing in their lies, in their false promises, in their endless calls for patience while they strip away everything we have fought for.

But this is the moment they never expected. The moment we stop trying. The moment we stop waiting. The moment we stop playing along. This is the moment we choose ourselves.

And if they do not change, if they refuse to evolve, if they refuse to dismantle the system that oppresses us, they will be left behind. Alone. Powerless. Forgotten. Because we are done. This is the final option. And we are ready.

Men Will Either Learn or Be Left Behind

The system that men built was always based on one assumption: that women would never leave. That no matter how much they took, no matter how much they exploited, no matter how much they abused, women would always stay. That we would endure. That we would continue to play the role they assigned to us, that we would keep trying to fix them, that we would sacrifice ourselves to uphold a system that has never served us. They believed that because we had always stayed, we always would. They confused our patience for acceptance, our resilience for submission, our ability to survive their world for agreement with its existence.

They assumed that even as they passed laws to strip us of our rights, even as they restricted our access to healthcare, even as they forced us to give birth against our will, even as they elevated rapists and abusers to power, even as they continued to burden us with unpaid labor and demand our loyalty while offering nothing in return, we would still be there. They assumed that we had nowhere else to go, that we had no alternative but to continue enduring, that we would never dare to simply walk away. But that assumption was their greatest mistake.

Because now, for the first time, women are leaving. Not just one or two. Not just the outliers, the radicals, the ones they dismissed as difficult or unnatural. Millions. Women are walking away from men, from marriage, from dating, from motherhood. Women are looking at the deal they were given and saying *no more.* Women are choosing themselves over a system that has only drained them, over relationships that have only benefited men, over an existence that has never been about their happiness, only about their utility. And the impact is beginning to show.

Marriage rates are plummeting because women are finally seeing marriage for what it truly is, a contract designed to benefit men, a lifetime of unpaid labor, a guarantee of emotional exhaustion, a structure in which women are expected to give everything and receive nothing. They are rejecting the idea that security means tying themselves to a man, rejecting the false promises of romance that too often turn into servitude. They are choosing freedom over tradition, autonomy over dependence, peace over the endless labor of fixing men who refuse to fix themselves.

Birth rates are declining because women are rejecting the notion that their purpose is to produce children for men, for the state, for capitalism. They are refusing to bring more life into a system that does not value them, that does not support them, that only punishes them for doing what men demand. They are choosing themselves over forced motherhood, over a lifetime of exhaustion, over a future in which they are expected to sacrifice everything for the sake of men who contribute nothing.

Fewer women are dating men at all because women have realized that most men offer them nothing but frustration, disappointment, and emotional labor. They are thriving without relationships. They are building lives that are full, complete, independent. They are no longer waiting for men to meet the bare minimum, no longer accepting mediocrity, no longer hoping that the next man will be different. Men, for the first time in history, are experiencing what women have always known: rejection.

They are feeling what it means to be left behind, to not be chosen, to watch as women move on without them. And their reaction? Panic. They call it a "crisis" when women refuse to marry. They call it a "problem" when birth rates fall. They create entire online communities dedicated to raging against women who no longer want them, blaming feminism, blaming independence, blaming everything but their own refusal to evolve. They push policies to punish women who do not conform, banning abortion, restricting contraception, attempting to legislate women back into submission. They do this because deep down, they know the truth.

They cannot survive without us. They need women to keep participating. They need us to be their caretakers, their emotional support systems, their unpaid labor force. They need us to keep giving, even as they refuse to change. And now, for the first time, we are done. If men want access to women's time, energy, and care, they will have to earn it. They will have to prove they are worth it. They will have to rebuild an entire system that was designed to exploit us, dismantle the structures that have kept us dependent, undo the damage they have inflicted for generations.

Because the world they created is no longer an option for us. We will not live under a system where we have fewer rights than our mothers, where our pain is ignored, where we are treated as disposable incubators for their next generation of oppressors. We will not stay in a world that was built for them at our expense.

So they have a choice. Change, or be left behind. They can learn to be equal partners, to dismantle the structures that oppress women, to earn the right to be in women's lives. Or they can watch as women build something new without them. Because women are no longer begging. We are not waiting. This is their final warning. And if they refuse to evolve? Then they will lose everything.

No More Dates, No More Sex, No More Marriage, No More Babies – Until We Win

We have given men every opportunity to change. We have explained, debated, educated, and begged. We have voted, marched, and fought for the right to exist as equals. We have shown them, again and again, the violence they inflict, the burdens they place upon us, the ways in which their power rests entirely on our oppression. And yet, they still refuse to listen. They still refuse to relinquish their entitlement, their control, their claim over our labor, our bodies, our futures. They have laughed in our faces, dismissed our demands, rolled back our rights, and expanded their power with no fear of consequence. They have assumed that we will continue to plead, continue to compromise, continue to tolerate their cruelty. They believe that no matter what they do, no matter how bad they make it for us, we will always stay. That no matter how much they take, we will always give. They believe we are trapped, that we have nowhere else to go, that their world is the only world. But they are wrong.

So now, we are making the choice for them. We are withdrawing our participation. We are refusing to be the foundation upon which they build their unchecked power. We are stepping back, walking away, cutting them off. No more dates. No more sex. No more marriage. No more babies. Until we win. This is not a demand, because we are done asking. This is not a negotiation, because we do not negotiate with those who refuse to see us as human. This is not a threat, because we owe them nothing, not even a warning. This is a decision. A final, irreversible decision. They have left us no choice but to fight them with the only weapon they cannot legislate away, our absence.

For too long, women have been taught that love, relationships, and family are the ultimate goal. That we must seek connection with men at all costs. That we must be forgiving, patient, and endlessly understanding, even when men refuse to evolve, refuse to learn, refuse to care. We have been told that suffering in the name of love is noble. That enduring mistreatment is part of womanhood. That to be alone is to be incomplete. But what have we received in return? Forced birth, abortion bans, attacks on contraception, all designed to keep us trapped, to ensure that we cannot escape their control. Rapists, abusers, pedophiles elevated to the highest offices, writing the very laws that govern our lives.

Marriage used as a cage, binding us to financial dependence, unpaid labor, and emotional exhaustion while men reap the benefits and contribute nothing. Motherhood turned into punishment, with no paid leave, no affordable childcare, no healthcare, only endless, thankless work. Through all of this, men have assumed that we will endure. That we will complain, protest, cry out, but in the end, we will stay. That we will still date them, still marry them, still birth their children, still build their world. They are wrong. We are done.

The strike has begun. Women are walking away, not as individuals, not as a fringe movement, but as a collective force. This is not a trend. This is not a phase. This is the dismantling of a system that only ever existed at our expense. No more dates. Men are not entitled to our time, our attention, our presence. No woman should waste another moment on a man who refuses to grow, refuses to contribute, refuses to offer more than the bare minimum. If they want a date, let them prove they deserve one.

Until then, they get nothing. No more sex. Sex has always been framed as something men get, and women give. They have built a world where their pleasure is prioritized, where women are expected to comply, where sex is an obligation rather than a choice. But women's bodies are not rewards for mediocre men. They are not services, not duties, not commodities to be taken for granted. Until men prove they respect women, that they are equal partners in intimacy, that they are worthy, there will be no more sex.

No more marriage. Marriage has never been about love. It has been about ownership. A contract that benefits men while leaving women drained, burdened, trapped. For generations, women were told that marriage was security. But security for whom? For men, who gain free labor, free emotional support, free caregiving? Women lose everything, time, money, independence. So now, we refuse. Until marriage is restructured into something that is truly equal, truly beneficial, truly free, we will not participate. No more babies. No more birthing the next generation of oppressors. No more bringing children into a world that does not support them. No more risking our lives in childbirth while men do nothing. They tell us we are selfish for refusing to have children. But what is selfish is demanding that women sacrifice everything while men contribute nothing. If men want children, let them fix the world first. Until then, the answer is simple: no.

Men can call it unfair. They can rage, panic, and try to legislate their way back into power. But none of it will work, because we are done playing their game. This is our final stand. No more dates. No more sex. No more marriage. No more babies. Until we win.

They will accuse us of destroying civilization, as if civilization was not built on our backs, as if it was not our labor, our suffering, our resilience that allowed them to thrive while we were left to struggle. They will say we are bitter, that we are vengeful, that we are misguided. They will try to turn our mothers against us, our sisters, our friends, reminding them of the so-called beauty of tradition, of family, of womanly duty. But they will not speak of the exhaustion, the degradation, the way those same women suffered in silence, the way they were discarded once they had given everything and had nothing left. They will not speak of the grandmothers who wasted away in marriages that drained them, of the mothers who died in childbirth because their pain was dismissed, of the sisters who were left to pick up the pieces when men abandoned their responsibilities. They will not admit that what they call civilization was always just control, control over our lives, our choices, our futures.

And when their words fail, when their shame tactics no longer work, when they realize that we are not bending, not breaking, not returning, they will turn to force. They will pass laws to trap us, criminalize our freedom, restrict our movement, punish our independence. They will use the state as a weapon, the church as a leash, the economy as a cage. They will push policies that incentivize marriage, punish single women, strip away our financial security. They will try to make it so that there is no world for us outside of them. But they will fail. Because we have learned. We have watched. We have studied history, and we see their desperation for what it is, a dying system gasping for air. And this time, we are not coming back to save it. They will either change, or they will be left behind. But we will be free.

Epilogue
The Last Word – And the Next Steps

What Happens When Millions of Women Opt Out?

The world does not function without women. This is the fundamental truth that men have always known but never admitted, the truth that lurks beneath their laws, their institutions, their religions, their desperate attempts to keep us tethered to them. They built their systems, marriage, family, the economy, the workforce, on one assumption: that women would always participate. That no matter how badly they treated us, no matter how many rights they stripped from us, no matter how much we suffered, we would continue to show up, continue to build, continue to sustain them. But what happens when we don't? What happens when millions of women stop dating, stop having sex, stop marrying, stop giving birth? What happens when we remove ourselves from the structures that have used us as fuel for centuries?

The system collapses.

Already, the first fractures are appearing. Birth rates are plummeting in countries where women's rights are under attack. Marriage rates are dropping as women realize they are better off alone. More women are choosing financial independence over domestic servitude, choosing community over the nuclear family, choosing themselves over a lifetime of unpaid labor. And men? They are panicking. They are writing desperate articles about the "marriage crisis," about declining birth rates, about the "epidemic" of single women who refuse to settle. They are scrambling for ways to drag women back into the roles they abandoned, passing laws to force childbirth, to limit women's freedom, to financially penalize those who refuse to participate. They are grasping at every possible mechanism of control because they know that once enough women say no, there is no going back. Once women withdraw from the system entirely, once they understand that they were never the ones who needed men but the other way around, the entire patriarchal order begins to unravel.

If women stop playing along, the impact is immediate. Men will no longer be able to coast through life, assuming that a woman will always be there to clean up their messes, to care for them, to fix them, to accommodate them. They will have to survive on their own, to meet the standards that women have always been held to. And they are woefully unprepared. For generations, they have built a world where their incompetence is excused, where their failures are cushioned by the labor of women, where they never had to be fully formed adults because there was always a woman to catch them when they fell. But when that safety net disappears, they will be left to fend for themselves in a world they never learned how to navigate.

Marriage will no longer be a default expectation. The notion that a woman must legally bind herself to a man to be seen as successful will vanish. Women will build independent lives, free from outdated traditions that only served to trap them. The economy will shift. When women stop prioritizing men's needs over their own, when they stop working for less, stop carrying the burden of unpaid domestic labor, stop making themselves small to accommodate men's egos, corporations, industries, and political structures that have relied on free female labor will be forced to adapt. Women will demand higher wages, better working conditions, economic policies that serve them, not men. And the pressure to have children will disappear. No longer will women be guilted into motherhood, expected to sacrifice their bodies, careers, and futures for a system that does not support them.

This is what scares them the most. Not just women saying no, but women thriving because of it. Women proving that they do not need husbands, do not need traditional families, do not need to be attached to men to live full, meaningful, successful lives. They fear not only being rejected but being forgotten.

They fear irrelevance. And once that truth becomes undeniable? Once women realize they never needed men at all?

The game is over. Because patriarchy was never built to withstand the moment women collectively walk away. It depends on us needing them more than they need us. But that was never true. They needed us. They still do. And now, for the first time, they have to earn us. Or they will lose us forever.

The Long Game – Permanent Structural Change

Opting out is just the beginning. Walking away from the men who refuse to evolve, refusing to participate in a system that exploits us, and choosing ourselves over servitude, this is the first step. But revolution is never merely about rejection. The act of refusal must be followed by reconstruction. To withdraw from the structures of patriarchy is not enough; we must ensure that these structures have no means of return, no avenue to resurrect themselves, no place to root themselves once more in our lives. The ultimate goal is not simply to escape but to annihilate the conditions that made our subjugation possible in the first place. We are not fighting for temporary relief; we are fighting for a future where no woman ever again has to wage this battle. A future where patriarchy does not merely decline, but ceases to exist as a viable system of power.

This is not about reforming a world that has already condemned us to suffering, it is about dismantling that world and building something new, something irreversible, something that ensures that the gains we make now will not be clawed back by the next generation of men who decide they have had enough of our autonomy. If we are to win, we must create a world where they have no way back, where our power is so absolute that the system that oppressed us becomes nothing but a historical relic, an unthinkable past.

The first mechanism of our oppression was economic dependence, and it must be the first thing we destroy. The world they built is designed to exploit women's unpaid labor, to drain us of time, energy, and resources while giving nothing in return. If they demand wives, girlfriends, and mothers, then they must pay for the labor they expect. No more unpaid caregiving, no more domestic servitude, no more financial burden falling on women while men coast through life without consequence. Women must seize control of their wealth, own their own homes, and build lives that are not tied to men's resources. If men are no longer needed for survival, they will no longer be able to leverage marriage and dependence as weapons of control.

We must build alternative economies, systems where women can rely on each other rather than on the unreliable promises of men. The less we need from them, the more irrelevant they become. And above all, we must end the expectation that women will carry the emotional burden of fixing men, healing them, and supporting them while receiving nothing in return. If men want access to women's time, labor, and love, they must give something real in return. And not the empty promise of future change, not the plea for endless patience while they remain stagnant, real, measurable, immediate transformation.

The world has conditioned us to believe that our purpose is to serve men, that our highest achievement is to be chosen by them. This lie has been reinforced through institutions, through religion, through socialization so deeply embedded that even women have believed it. But once women refuse to play this role, once they remove men as the center of their lives, everything shifts. The strongest, most reliable relationships in most women's lives have always been with other women. Sisterhood is not an alternative to male validation, it is the foundation of something much stronger.

Women must prioritize these bonds over the fleeting, conditional relationships they have been trained to seek from men. The definition of success must be rewritten. No longer will women be measured by whether they have married or borne children, but by the lives they build for themselves. Independence, creativity, freedom, these will be the new markers of fulfillment. We will raise a generation of daughters who know they owe men nothing, who do not measure their worth by male approval, who do not believe that their role is to fix or tolerate. We will teach them what we have only just begun to understand, that walking away is not failure, it is power.

Men created a world where they enjoyed all the power and bore none of the responsibility. They assumed women would always be there, dating them, marrying them, raising their children, no matter how little they offered in return. They were wrong. The balance has shifted. If men want access to women, they will have to earn it. They will have to prove they are equals, prove they are worthy. And it will no longer be enough to simply be better than the worst; the standard has changed.

There will be no more bare minimum. No more rewarding men for simply not being monsters. They will be equal partners, emotional contributors, and engaged participants in relationships, or they will be alone. The time of tolerating mediocrity is over. Women will no longer waste their lives teaching men how to be decent human beings. Either they figure it out on their own, or they are left behind. No more second chances. No more waiting for them to catch up. They have had centuries. If they refuse to change, they will be made irrelevant.

We do not wait for men to change. We do not beg, we do not plead, we do not ask permission. We change the world so that they have no choice but to keep up or disappear. And once that happens, there is no going back. There is no return to the world they built, no return to the comfort of our unpaid labor, no return to a system that let them reign unchallenged while we suffered in silence. The moment women refuse, the moment we reject the game entirely, the moment we make it clear that their participation in our lives is optional, patriarchy dies. And when it does, it will not be mourned. It will not be revived. It will not be rebuilt. It will be buried alongside every other failed empire that believed it could last forever.

The Moment We Say No, We Win

They have built a world in which we are necessary but never valued, essential but never respected. They have constructed an entire civilization on the silent, unpaid, unrecognized labor of women, yet they pretend as though it is men who have carried the burden of history. They have written laws, designed religions, shaped economies, all with the singular purpose of ensuring that women remain bound, controlled, servile. And they have done this not because they believe in their own superiority, not because they see themselves as rightful rulers, but because they know the truth, their power is fragile, their dominance is an illusion, and without women to uphold them, they are nothing.

They dress their authority in the language of tradition, in the veneer of divine order, in the manufactured logic of biological determinism, but beneath it all is fear. They fear what happens when women are no longer afraid, when we no longer believe in the necessity of their rule, when we step beyond the boundaries they have so carefully constructed. They do not fear our inferiority; they fear our liberation. Because once we stop serving them, once we stop carrying the weight of their world, they will be forced to carry themselves, and they know they are incapable.

They cling to the past because they know that the future, if left unshackled, does not belong to them. The weight of their history, of their violence, their oppression, their greed, looms over them, and they fear what will happen when women stop forgiving, stop excusing, stop bearing their burdens without protest. They fear a world in which women do not exist to soothe their egos, to raise their sons, to serve as quiet witnesses to their mediocrity. They know that when women refuse, when women walk away, the entire foundation they have built for themselves begins to tremble.

This is why their response is always rage, always coercion, always brutality. They do not know how to exist in a world where women are not theirs to possess. They react with desperation, with new laws restricting our autonomy, with renewed cries for "traditional values," with violence in the streets and in our homes. They beg us to come back with one hand while tightening their grip with the other. But they do not realize that their fear no longer moves us. That their threats no longer hold power. That we have already made our choice.

For centuries, they have relied on the idea that women's compliance is inevitable. They believed that women would always endure, that we would always return, that no matter how much they took, we would continue to give. They assumed that our capacity for suffering was infinite. They mistook our patience for acceptance, our resilience for submission, our ability to love for an inability to revolt. They have watched women bleed, struggle, die under the weight of their system, and they have never once imagined that we might stop carrying it. But now we have.

Now, women are walking away, not in anger, not in protest, but in simple, unshakable certainty. We no longer explain ourselves. We no longer engage in the debate. We no longer wait for men to understand what they have always known but refused to acknowledge, that without women, their world does not function. That without women, they have no future. And the fear that has always belonged to us now belongs to them.

We are no longer pleading. We are no longer educating them, trying to make them understand. We are no longer appealing to their morality, waiting for them to awaken to the injustice of their own making. They have proven, time and time again, that they are incapable of change. That they would rather burn the world down than share it. That they would rather strip us of our rights, of our agency, of our dignity, than relinquish even a fraction of their control. But the moment women understand that we do not have to participate, the moment we recognize that our withdrawal is more powerful than our resistance, their world begins to collapse. The moment we see that their power is not real, that it exists only because we allow it to exist, we dismantle it without lifting a single weapon.

We are rejecting the roles they assigned us. We are turning away from their institutions, their traditions, their demands. No more marriages that serve as contracts of ownership. No more children born into a world that does not deserve them. No more service to men who see us as disposable. No more. They will call us selfish. They will call us unnatural. They will call us every name they have created to shame women back into submission. But their words mean nothing. Their insults are hollow. Their rage is impotent.

They know this because they can see what is coming, a world that does not revolve around them, a world in which women are free in ways they have never been, a world where they are not needed, not feared, not even considered. And it is not hatred that fuels this exodus, it is indifference. Women no longer need to destroy men. We simply no longer need to acknowledge them.

This is not a revolution of violence but a revolution of refusal. We do not have to fight them to defeat them. We only have to walk away. Let them legislate, let them rage, let them beg for the return of a system that only ever benefited them. It is too late. We are leaving, and we are never coming back.

Special Note

Why do they hate us so much? Because they fear us

Men have always feared women, though they would never admit it. They have masked that fear behind laws, behind violence, behind the centuries-long effort to reduce women to objects, to incubators, to nameless bodies that serve but do not speak. They have called us irrational, hysterical, weak. They have said we are unfit for power, unworthy of autonomy, too fragile for leadership. But their fear is evident not in their words but in their actions. You do not build entire civilizations around the subjugation of something that is not a threat. You do not pass law after law restricting the freedom of those you claim are unimportant. You do not rewrite history, erase women's names, silence their voices, and burn their knowledge unless you are terrified of what they might do with that power. If women were truly inferior, there would be no need for all these chains. No need for the constant surveillance, the forced pregnancies, the manufactured dependence. They fear what we will become when we are no longer under their control.

And they should.

They hate us because they know they are nothing without us. They hate us because we see them clearly, stripped of the mythologies they have built around themselves. They are weak. They are fragile. They do not know how to survive without the quiet endurance of women, without our labor, our patience, our willingness to suffer so that they may thrive. Their entire system depends on the silent sacrifices of women who raise their children, manage their homes, support their ambitions, absorb their rage, forgive their failures, clean up their messes. Without us, they collapse. And that collapse is coming. The moment women step back, withdraw their energy, refuse to play their game, the entire structure built on our backs begins to shake. And that is why they rage. That is why they legislate.

That is why they kill. Because they know that if women stop, everything stops.

They call us unnatural for refusing to marry, for refusing to bear children, for refusing to dedicate our lives to their comfort. But what is unnatural is forcing half the population into servitude while the other half takes and takes without consequence. What is unnatural is denying women bodily autonomy, trapping them in violent marriages, treating them as property, and then expecting them to remain compliant forever. They have spent centuries gaslighting women into believing that oppression is love, that suffering is noble, that their worth is determined by their ability to serve men. But now, the illusion is breaking. Women are waking up, walking away, choosing themselves. And men are panicking.

Because the greatest fear of every oppressor is that one day, the oppressed will realize they do not have to comply. And when that realization spreads, when women everywhere stop tolerating, stop enduring, stop sacrificing themselves for men who have given them nothing, the power balance shifts permanently. That is what keeps them up at night. That is why they are scrambling to force us back into submission. They know that once we understand our power, we will never go back.

And what happens then? What happens when women stop birthing the next generation of oppressors, stop marrying men who do not respect them, stop tolerating mediocrity, stop accepting the bare minimum? What happens when they look at the system men built and say, no more? Men will finally feel what women have felt for centuries, powerlessness. They will experience the terror of knowing they are no longer wanted, no longer necessary, no longer in control. And it will be their own fault. Because women did not destroy them, they destroyed themselves. They refused to evolve..They refused to see women as equals. They chose their own entitlement over survival.

So let them fear us. Let them hate us. Let them try to fight a battle they have already lost. We are not coming back. We are not giving in. We are not waiting anymore. Like the tide, we are rising.

They should be afraid. Enough is enough.

List of Prints

About EATMS Productions

What's happening to women now is not random. It's structural.

Policy, culture, technology, and power are moving in the same direction.

EATMS maps them clearly and shows how to respond.

This title is part of an ongoing body of work. All EATMS Productions titles, across all series, authors, and formats, are components of a single connected project.

Start here: EATMS System Primer — Free Bundle
https://eatms.gumroad.com/l/dyvzbw

For full catalog or inquiries: eatms.me

Free survival booklet + EATMS updates: email "EATMS" to eatms@pm.me

Please feel free to burn part or all of this book, safely, as an effigy.

www.ingramcontent.com/pod-product-compliance
Lightning Source LLC
LaVergne TN
LVHW051001080826
845145LV00009B/2389
* 9 7 8 1 9 6 6 0 1 4 1 1 9 *